# MARQUEE MESSAGES

# MARQUEE MESSAGES

## Sentence Sermons for the Church Sign

# Shirley Jones Garmon

Book Editor: Wanda Griffith
Editorial Assistant: Tammy Hatfield
Copy Editors: Cresta Shawver
Oreeda Burnette
Inside Layout: Mark Shuler


Library of Congress Catalog Card Number: 00-111637
ISBN: 0-87148-613-X
Copyright © 2000 by Pathway Press
Cleveland, Tennessee 37311
All Rights Reserved
Printed in the United States of America

# DEDICATION

To my daughters,

*Marissa* and *Whitney*,

who are the sunshine of my life.


To my mom and dad,

*Ted* and *Claudia Jones*,

who have been the greatest sources
of wisdom and example.


And to my husband,

*Fred*,

for his constant encouragement.

# TABLE OF CONTENTS

# PREFACE

This book has resulted from the many years my husband and I have pastored and searched for ways to reach the lost and encourage Christians. In 1988 while pastoring a church in Southwest Florida, we purchased a new church sign. That's when my search began to find proverbs and sentence sermons to fill the marquee each week. After visiting several bookstores, both Christian and secular, I found no resources. Since that time I have been collecting proverbs.

I have found them in bulletins, newspapers, bumper stickers, the Bible, on other church marquees, sermons, songs, on billboards, on T-shirts, at craft shows, on the Internet, and many have been sent to me through e-mail. It is impossible to trace each proverb to its originator. It is not my intention to profit from anyone else's material—I simply want to provide a resource so that churches and pastors can communicate the gospel more effectively.

# CALENDAR

Four weekly messages to choose from including a scripture per week.

## JANUARY

### 1st Week

Have your faith lifted here!

No matter what your past, your future is spotless.

When you flee temptation,
don't leave a forwarding address.

"In all your ways acknowledge Him, and He shall
direct your path" (Proverbs 3:6, *NKJV*).

### 2nd Week

Dusty Bibles lead to dirty lives.

Horse sense comes from a stable mind.

If God is kept outside, something is wrong inside.

God calls you His friend.

### 3rd Week

He who throws dirt loses ground.

Fight truth decay—study the Bible daily.

"Injustice anywhere is a threat
to justice everywhere."—M.L. King Jr.

"All things work together for good
to them that love God" (Romans 8:28).

### 4th Week

Let's meet at my house
Sunday before the game.—God

Got Jesus?

Today is not won by old victories,
nor lost by old defeats.

"I will never leave thee, nor forsake thee"
(Hebrews 13:5).

# FEBRUARY

### 1st Week

22FEB2015 NOONE

You can't hide from God by missing church.

If the going is getting easier, you aren't climbing.

A chip on the shoulder indicates
there is wood higher up.

God measures us by our hearts, not our heads.

## 2nd Week

Put your spouse first so your marriage will last.

A happy marriage is the union of two good forgivers. 15ᴺᵒᵛ2014

God can heal a broken heart,
but He has to have all the pieces.

Love doesn't keep score.

## 3rd Week

Anger manages everything badly.

The end never justifies the means.

Don't wait till you get to heaven
to start acting like an angel.

"Be rich in good works" (1 Timothy 6:18).

## 4th Week

Daily prayer diminishes your cares.

Do not wait for the hearse to take you to church.

Today is a gift . . . that's why it's called "the present."

"Love your enemies" (Matthew 5:44).

# MARCH

### 1st Week

Forbidden fruit creates many jams.

When there is pruning, the Gardener is nearby.

God should be our steering wheel, not our spare tire.

"A soft answer turneth away wrath" (Proverbs 15:1).

## 2nd Week

In trying times, don't quit trying.

Feed your faith and your doubts will starve to death.

Too many people miss the silver lining
because they're expecting gold.

"To everything there is a season, a time to every
purpose" (Ecclesiastes 3:1, *NKJV*).

## 3rd Week

Life is fragile, handle with prayer.

A man wrapped up in himself
makes a very small package.

There is a place for people with no problems.
It's called the cemetery.

"A happy heart makes
the face cheerful" (Proverbs 15:13, *NIV*).

## 4th Week

Every Sunday is OPEN HOUSE.

You were created to be an answer.

He who buries his talent is making a grave mistake.

"A good name is rather to be chosen than great
riches" (Proverbs 22:1).

### 5th Week

Free trip to heaven—details inside.

You never see a fish on the wall
with its mouth shut.

A pessimist always complains about the noise
when opportunity knocks.

"Thou shalt not avenge" (Leviticus 19:18).

# APRIL

### 1st Week

Sign broken—message inside this Sunday.

Judge this day not by the harvest
but by the seeds planted.

The closer we are to the Shepherd,
the farther we are from the wolf.

"A fool says in his heart,
'There is no God'" (Psalm 14:1). 28DEC2014

### 2nd Week

"Into each life some rain must fall."—Longfellow

Floating members make a sinking church.

Today is the tomorrow
you worried about yesterday.

They'll know you are Christians by your love.

### 3rd Week

It's better to give than to deceive (the IRS).

It is unlikely there'll be a reduction
in the wages of sin.

Conscience is the inner voice that tells you
the IRS might audit your return.

"Fear not: for I am with thee" (Isaiah 43:5).

### 4th Week

Easter, the rest of the Christmas story.

Nails didn't keep Jesus on the cross,
love held Him there.

Jesus rose from the dead, you can get up out of
the bed, Easter Sunday, 10 a.m.

"For God so loved the world that he gave His only
begotten Son that whosoever believeth in him
should have everlasting life" (John 3:16).

# MAY

### 1st Week

Prayer is the pause that empowers.

A smile is a little curve that makes things straight.

A mighty oak was once a little nut
that stood his ground!

"Blessed are the peacemakers" (Matthew 5:9).

## 2nd Week

An ounce of mother is worth more
than a pound of clergy.

"A foolish man despises his mother"
(Proverbs 15:20).

"The best gift a father can give his children is to
love their mother" (Ephesians 5:25).

"Honor your father and your mother"
(Exodus 20:12, *NKJV*).

## 3rd Week

You may be in the driver's seat,
but God holds the map.

Shoot for the moon.  Even if you miss,
you'll be among stars.

When our course is controlled by God,
we soar to heights never imagined.

"I can do all things through Christ which
strengtheneth me" (Philippians 4:13).

## 4th Week

In the dark?  Follow the Son.  15 Nov 2014

God will supply that for which we have "knee'd."

War does not determine who is right,
only who is left.

"A faithful man shall abound with blessings"
(Proverbs 28:20).

# JUNE

## 1st Week

Worry is the misuse of imagination.

A man without principle never draws much interest.

You can't act like a skunk without
someone getting wind of it.

"Call upon me in the day of trouble: I will deliver
thee" (Psalm 50:15).

## 2nd Week

The password to eternity is JESUS.

Those prepared to die are the most prepared to live.

You're not too bad to come to church
or too good to stay away.

Forgiveness means giving up your rights to revenge.

## 3rd Week

The best inheritance a father can leave
is a good example.

Thank God for fathers who not only gave us life,
but who also taught us how to live.

Remember when we honored father and mother
instead of all the major credit cards.

Hear the instruction of your father
and get understanding.

### 4th Week

Never take a vacation from God.

Skipping church is the beginning
of spiritual decline.

Spiritual food is needed in hot weather
as well as in cool.

"There is a friend that sticketh
closer than a brother" (Proverbs 18:24).

### 5th Week

What would Jesus do?

The company you keep will determine
the trouble you meet.

The right train of thought can take you
to a better station in life.

"The steps of a good man are ordered by the Lord"
(Psalm 37:23).

# JULY

### 1st Week

God knows our history and our future.

A nation is only as good as the people in it.

A people that values their privileges
over their principles soon loses both.

"Righteousness exalteth a nation" (Proverbs 14:34).

## 2nd Week

God is in control.

Walk close to God so nothing
can come between.

Try our Sundays—they're better
than Baskin Robbins.

"Whatsoever a man soweth,
that shall he also reap" (Galatians 6:7).

## 3rd Week

Turn your stumbling blocks
into stepping stones.

The world needs more warm hearts
and fewer hot heads.

There is nothing like a cool refreshing drink
from the Word of God.

"Pride goes before destruction"
(Proverbs 16:18, *NIV*).

## 4th Week

Kindness is timeless.

A shut mouth gathers no foot.

The thickest clouds often bring
the heaviest showers of blessings.

"A friend loves at all times"
(Proverbs 17:17, *NKJV*).

# AUGUST

## 1st Week

You think it's hot here?—God

Be as patient with others as God is with you.

The sin we try to cover up
will eventually bring us down.

"We ought to obey God
rather than men" (Acts 5:29).

## 2nd Week

Study hard for school; pray hard for life.

God buries our sins and doesn't mark the grave.

A Christian without a church
is like a bee without a hive.

If you wait for perfect conditions,
you'll never get anything done.

## 3rd Week

OPEN HOUSE every Sunday 11 a.m.

Most arguments are caused by
the wrong tone of voice.

Mental-floss regularly with God's Word
to avoid truth decay.

"A double-minded man is unstable in all his ways"
(James 1:8).

### 4th Week

We need to talk.—God

A happy heart is better than a full purse.

Opportunity knocks only once,
but temptation leans on the doorbell.

"With God all things are possible"
(Matthew 19:26).

# SEPTEMBER

### 1st Week

Children need models more
than they need critics.

Kindness is the oil that takes
the friction out of life.

Be like the tea kettle—sing when
you're in hot water up to your nose.

"Whosoever shall call on the name of the Lord
shall be saved" (Acts 2:21).

### 2nd Week

Soft words are hard arguments.

God plus one is always a majority.

A day outlined in prayer is less likely to unravel.

"Whosoever putteth his trust in the Lord
shall be safe" (Proverbs 29:25).

### 3rd Week

Decision determines destiny.

If you think education is
expensive, try ignorance.

A coincidence is a small miracle
where God prefers to be anonymous.

"They that wait upon the Lord shall
renew their strength" (Isaiah 40:31).

### 4th Week

Success is failure turned inside out.

Fight truth decay—study the Bible daily.

When you're facing God, *21 JUN 2015*
your back is to the world.

"The Lord is nigh unto them that are
of a broken heart" (Psalm 34:18).

### 5th Week

The bread of life makes you grow.

Others will follow your footsteps
quicker than your advice.

Watch out for temptation; the more you
see of it, the better it looks.

"The eternal God is thy refuge"
(Deuteronomy 33:27).

# OCTOBER

## 1st Week

Love is a language anyone can speak.

The only way to walk without falling
is on your knees.

If you stand in the middle of the road,
you'll get knocked down by both sides.

Not one word of His promises has failed.

## 2nd Week

Good manners are made up of petty sacrifices.

We may not always agree with God,
but He is still the Boss.

If your religion doesn't take you to church,
it's doubtful it will take you to heaven.

"If you forgive men their trespasses,
your heavenly Father will also forgive you"
(Matthew 6:14, *NKJV*).

## 3rd Week

The more you grow up, the less you blow up.

If you're heading in the wrong direction, ~~11/9/2014~~
God allows U-turns.

If you can't sleep, don't count sheep . . .
talk to the Shepherd.

If you can be faithful in a few things,
God will give you rule over many.

24

### 4th Week

Practice random acts of kindness.

An atheist is a man who has
no invisible means of support.

Prayer should be the key of the morning
and the lock of the night.

"I will never leave thee, nor forsake thee"
(Hebrews 13:5).

# NOVEMBER

### 1st Week

Faithfulness in little things is a great thing.

An ounce of example is worth a pound of advice. 19 oct 2014

An argument is the longest distance 25 oct 2014
between two points.

"God is our refuge and strength, a very present
help in trouble" (Psalm 46:1).

### 2nd Week

Prayer lubricates the machinery of life.

Pressure turns a lump of coal into a diamond.

Tomorrow's challenges
are already on God's agenda.

"He that is of a merry of heart hath
a continual feast" (Proverbs 15:15).

### 3rd Week

"In everything give thanks"
(1 Thessalonians 5:18, *NKJV*).

Have an attitude of gratitude.

A thankful heart is the parent of all virtues.

God measures us by our hearts,
not our heads.

### 4th Week

Ingratitude is the daughter of pride.

Ingratitude is the mother of every vice.

Too busy adding up your troubles
to count your blessings?

"Forgive, and ye shall be forgiven" (Luke 6:37).

# DECEMBER

### 1st Week

Miracles happen!

Drinking is committing suicide
on the installment plan.

If your mind goes blank,
be sure to turn off the sound.

"His love endures forever"
(Psalm 136:1, *NIV*).

## 2nd Week

Advice when most needed is least heeded.

An apology is a good way to have the last word. ⟶ 11/2/2014

A Christian heart is a good thing . . .
a Christian liver is much better.

"He shall give his angels
charge over thee" (Psalm 91:11).

## 3rd Week

Wise men still seek Him today.

Jesus is the reason for the season.

Don't leave CHRIST out of CHRISTmas.

"Lo, I am with you always, even unto
the end of the age" (Matthew 28:20, *NKJV*).

## 4th Week

Let your resolution be His solution.

Heaven; don't miss it for the world!

You never stand taller than
when you kneel before God.

"Whatsoever good thing any man doeth,
the same shall he receive" (Ephesians 6:8).

# SCRIPTURES

Some churches prefer to only use Scriptures on their signs. This section includes a list of short and to-the-point scriptures; some are a portion of a verse in order to fit one thought on the marquee.

"A double minded man is unstable in all his ways" (James 1:8).

"A faithful man shall abound with blessings" (Proverbs 28:20).

"A foolish man despises his mother" (Proverbs 15:20, *NKJV*).

"A friend loves at all times" (Proverbs 17:17, *NIV*).

"A good name is better than precious ointment" (Ecclesiastes 7:1).

"A good name is rather to be chosen than great riches" (Proverbs 22:1).

"A happy heart makes the face cheerful" (Proverbs 15:13, *NIV*).

"A merry heart doeth good like a medicine" (Proverbs 17:22).

"A soft answer turneth away wrath"
(Proverbs 15:1).

"A soft answer turns away wrath, but harsh words
cause quarrels" (Proverbs 15:1, *TLB*).

"A soft tongue can break hard bones"
(Proverbs 25:15, *TLB*).

"A wise man doesn't display his knowledge,
but a fool displays his foolishness"
(Proverbs 12:23, *TLB*).

"A wise son brings joy to his father"
(Proverbs 15:20, *NIV*).

"All things work together for good to them
that love God" (Romans 8:28).

"Any story sounds true until someone tells
the other side and sets the record straight"
(Proverbs 18:17, *TLB*).

"Be faithful until death, and I will give you
the crown of life" (Revelation 2:10, *NKJV*).

"Be rich in good works" (1 Timothy 6:18).

"Be sure your sin will find you out" (Numbers 32:23).

"Before every man there lies a wide and pleasant
road he thinks is right, but it ends in death"
(Proverbs 16:25, *TLB*).

"Blessed are the merciful: for they shall
obtain mercy" (Matthew 5:7).

"Blessed are the peacemakers" (Matthew 5:9).

"Blessed are the pure in heart: for they shall
see God" (Matthew 5:8).

"Blessed be the Lord, who daily loadeth us
with benefits" (Psalm 68:19).

"Call unto me, and I will answer thee"
(Jeremiah 33:3).

"Call upon me in the day of trouble:
I will deliver thee" (Psalm 50:15).

"Cast all your care on Him;
for he cares for you" (1 Peter 5:7).

"Cast thy burden upon the Lord, and He
shall sustain thee" (Psalm 55:22).

"Do not love sleep or you will grow poor"
(Proverbs 20:13).

"Do not repay anyone evil for evil"
(Romans 12:17, *NIV*).

"Do to others what you would have them
do to you" (Matthew 7:12, *NIV*).

"Draw near to God and He will draw near to You"
(James 4:8, *NKJV*).

"Even a child is known by his doings" 11 oCT 2014
(Proverbs 20:11).

"Faith without works is dead" (James 2:26).

"Fear not: for I am with thee" (Isaiah 43:5).

"Fire goes out for lack of fuel, and tensions disap-
pear when gossip stops" (Proverbs 26:20, *TLB*).

"Forgive, and ye shall be forgiven" (Luke 6:37).

"From a wise mind comes careful and persuasive
speech" (Proverbs 16:23, *TLB*).

"God is a refuge for us" (Psalm 62:8).

"God is able to make all grace abound toward you"
(2 Corinthians 9:8).

"God is our refuge and strength, a very present
help in trouble" (Psalm 46:1).

"God is with thee in all that thou doest"
(Genesis 21:22).

"God shall wipe away all tears" (Revelation 21:4).

"Godliness exalts a nation, but sin is a reproach to
any people" (Proverbs 14:34, *TLB*).

"Gossip separates the best of friends"
(Proverbs 16:28, *TLB*).

"Great peace have they which love thy law"
(Psalm 119:165).

"Happy are the people whose God is the Lord"
(Psalm 144:15, *NKJV*).

"Hatred stirs up strife; but love covers all sins"
(Proverbs 10:12, *NKJV*).

"He heals the brokenhearted, and binds up
their wounds" (Psalm 147:3, *NKJV*).

"He shall give his angels charge over thee"
(Psalm 91:11).

"He that believeth on me hath everlasting life"
(John 6:47).

"He that dwelleth in love dwelleth in God,
and God in him" (1 John 4:16).

"He that dwelleth in the secret place of
the Most High shall abide under
the shadow of the Almighty" (Psalm 91:1).

"He who follows Me shall not walk in darkness"
(John 8:12, *NKJV*).

"He that is of a merry of heart hath
a continual feast" (Proverbs 15:15).

"He that is without sin, let him cast
the first stone" (John 8:7).

"He that loses his life for [Jesus'] sake
shall find it" (Matthew 10:39).

"He which soweth bountifully shall
reap also bountifully" (2 Corinthians 9:6).

"He who humbles himself will be exalted"
(Matthew 23:12, *NKJV*).

"Heaven and earth shall pass away, but my words
shall not pass away" (Matthew 24:35).

"Honesty is its own defense" (Proverbs 12:13, *TLB*).

"Humble yourselves in the sight of the Lord, and
he shall lift you up" (James 4:10).

"I can do all things through Christ which
strengtheneth me" (Philippians 4:13).

"I will go before thee, and make the crooked
places straight" (Isaiah 45:2).

"I will never leave thee, nor forsake thee"
(Hebrews 13:5).

"Idle hands are the devil's workshop; idle lips
are his mouthpiece" (Proverbs 16:27, *TLB*).

"If my people . . . will humble themselves, and pray
. . . I will heal their land" (2 Chronicles 7:14, *NKJV*).

"If you ask anything in My name,
I will do it" (John 14:14, *NKJV*).

"If you forgive others their trespasses, your heavenly Father will also forgive you" (Matthew 6:14).

"Ill-gotten gain brings no lasting happiness; right living does" (Proverbs 10:2, *TLB*).

"In all your ways acknowledge Him, and He shall direct your paths" (Proverbs 3:6, *NKJV*).

"In the multitude of counselors there is safety" (Proverbs 11:14).

"It is better to have self-control than to control an army" (Proverbs 16:32, *TLB*).

"It is more blessed to give than to receive" (Acts 20:35).

"It is possible to give away and become richer!" (Proverbs 11:24, *TLB*).

"It is also possible to hold on too tightly and lose everything" (Proverbs 11:24, *TLB*).

"He must increase; I must decrease" (John 3:30).

"Kind words are like honey—enjoyable and healthy" (Proverbs 16:24, *TLB*).

"Lazy men are soon poor; hard workers get rich" (Proverbs 10:4, *TLB*).

"Death and life are in the power of the tongue" (Proverbs 18:21).

"Lo, I am with you alway, even unto the end of the world" (Matthew 28:20).

"Love your enemies" (Matthew 5:44).

"Lying lips are an abomination to the Lord" (Proverbs 12:22, *NKJV*).

"Many waters cannot quench love, neither can the floods drown it" (Song of Solomon 8:7).

"My God shall supply all your need according to His riches in glory" (Philippians 4:19).

"My grace is sufficient for thee" (2 Corinthians 12:9).

"My help comes from the Lord, which made heaven and earth" (Psalm 121:2).

"No man can serve two masters" (Matthew 6:24).

"No weapon formed against you shall prosper" (Isaiah 54:17).

"Only a fool idles away his time" (Proverbs 12:11, *TLB*).

"Our days on the earth are as a shadow" (1 Chronicles 29:15).

"Out of the abundance of the heart the mouth speaketh" (Matthew 12:34).

"Peace I leave with you, My peace I give unto you" (John 14:27).

"Pride goes before destruction, and a haughty spirit before a fall" (Proverbs 16:18, *NKJV*).

"Righteousness exalteth a nation" (Proverbs 14:34).

"Silver and gold are purified by fire, but God purifies hearts" (Proverbs 17:3, *TLB*).

"Teach a child to choose the right path, and when he is older he will remain upon it" (Proverbs 22:6, *TLB*).

"The eternal God is thy refuge" (Deuteronomy 33:27).

"The eyes of the Lord are over the righteous, and His ears are open unto their prayers" (1 Peter 3:12).

"The first to present his case seems right, till
another comes forward and questions him"
(Proverbs 18:17, *NIV*).

"The fool has said in his heart,
'There is no God'" (Psalm 14:1).

"The good influence of godly citizens causes a city
to prosper" (Proverbs 11:11, *TLB*).

"The just shall live by faith" (Romans 1:17).

"The Lord blesses good men and
condemns the wicked" (Proverbs 12:2, *TLB*).

"The Lord is nigh unto them that are
of a broken heart" (Psalm 34:18).

"The Lord raiseth them that are bowed down"
(Psalm 146:8).

"The Lord shall open unto thee His good treasure"
(Deuteronomy 28:12).

"A tree is known by its fruit" (Matthew 12:33, *NKJV*). 08 MAR 2015

"The wicked accuse; the godly defend"
(Proverbs 12:6, *TLB*).

"The wise man is glad to be instructed,
but a self-sufficient fool falls flat
on his face" (Proverbs 10:8, *TLB*).

"The word of the Lord endureth forever"
(1 Peter 1:25).

"There is a friend that sticketh closer
than a brother" (Proverbs 18:24).

"They that wait upon the Lord shall
renew their strength" (Isaiah 40:31).

"Those that seek Me early shall find Me"
(Proverbs 8:17).

"Thou shalt not avenge" (Leviticus 19:18).

"Thou wilt keep him in perfect peace, whose mind
is stayed on thee" (Isaiah 26:3).

"Though I walk in the midst of trouble, thou wilt
revive me" (Psalm 138:7).

"To everything there is a season; a time
to every purpose" (Ecclesiastes 3:1).

"To learn, you must want to be taught"
(Proverbs 12:1, *TLB*).

"Train up a child in the way he should go: and
when he is old, he will not depart from it"
(Proverbs 22:6).

"Truth stands the test of time; lies are
soon exposed" (Proverbs 12:19, *TLB*).

"We can make our plans, but the final outcome
is in God's hands" (Proverbs 16:1, *TLB*).

"We walk by faith, not by sight" (2 Corinthians 5:7).

"What shall it profit a man, if he shall gain the
whole world, and lose his own soul?" (Mark 8:36).

"Whatsoever a man soweth, that shall
he also reap" (Galatians 6:7).

"Whatsoever good thing any man doeth, the same
shall he receive" (Ephesians 6:8).

"Whom the Lord loveth
He correcteth" (Proverbs 3:12).

"Whosoever putteth his trust in the Lord
shall be safe" (Proverbs 29:25).

"Whosoever believeth in Him shall receive remission of sins" (Acts 10:43).

"Whosoever shall call on the name of the Lord shall be saved" (Acts 2:21).

"With God all things are possible" (Matthew 19:26).

"Without faith it is impossible to please God" (Hebrews 11:6).

"Your heavenly Father knoweth that ye have need of all these things" (Matthew 6:32).

"Your riches won't help you on Judgment Day; only righteousness counts then" (Proverbs 11:4, *TLB*).

# ADVERSITY

Adversity can destroy you or make
you strong. It's your choice.

Adversity causes some men to break
and others to break records.

Adversity introduces a man to himself.

Adversity is fertile soil for creativity.

Adversity tests integrity.

Difficult situations do not make heroes or
cowards, they simply unveil them.

Don't let adversity get you down
unless you are on your knees.

In prosperity friends know us; in
adversity we know our friends.

Prosperity makes friends; adversity tries them.

Prosperity tries the fortunate; adversity, the great.

Sometimes we need to recognize ourselves
as the sole cause of our adversity.

There is no education like adversity.

We can have our best witness in the worst of times.

What we call adversity, God calls opportunity.

Adversity

When in trouble, some people grow wings;
others buy crutches.

# ANGER AND HATRED

"A soft answer turneth away
wrath" (Proverbs 15:1).

"A soft answer turns away wrath, but harsh words
cause quarrels" (Proverbs 15:1, *TLB*).

An argument is the longest
distance between two points.

Anger is a bad counselor.

Anger is a mask that hides insecurity.

Anger makes your mouth work
faster than your mind.

Anger punishes itself.

Character is revealed by your
actions in an unguarded moment.

Don't blow up, grow up!

Don't ever slam the door; you
might want to go back.

For every minute you're angry, you
lose 60 seconds of happiness.

Hatred is a coward's revenge for being intimidated.

Hatred is a prolonged form of
suicide of your dreams.

"Hatred stirs up strife; but love
covers all sins" (Proverbs 10:12, *NKJV*).

Hatred watches while friendship sleeps.

"Your Word is a lamp to my feet and
a light for my path" (Psalm 119:105, *NIV*).

Most arguments are caused by
the wrong tone of voice.

Silence is one of the hardest things to refute.

Swallowing angry words is easier than eating them.

The best measure of a person's mentality is
the significance of the things he will argue about.

The greatest remedy for anger is delay.

The man who loses his head is
usually the last to miss it.

The more you grow up, the less you blow up.

The world needs more warm
hearts and fewer hot heads.

Think, then speak.

Two wrongs do not make a right.

You can disagree without being disagreeable.

# THE BIBLE

A Bible in hand is worth two on the shelf.

A home without a Bible is like
a ship without a compass.

Dusty Bibles lead to dirty lives.

Fight truth decay—study the Bible daily.

"Your Word is a lamp to our feet and a light for
my path" (Psalm 119:105, *NIV*).

"It is impossible to govern the world without God
and the Bible."—George Washington

Knowing Scripture is one thing;
knowing the Author is another.

Mental floss regularly with God's

Word to avoid truth decay.

Most books are given for information;
the Bible was given for transformation.

One evidence of the value of the Bible is the
character of those who oppose it.

One revealed truth from the Bible is worth
more than all the wisdom of men.

Reading the Bible is to the mind
what exercise is to the body.

Sin will keep you from the Bible,
but the Bible will keep you from sin.

Study without reflection is a waste of time;
reflection without study is dangerous!

The best stress tablet you can
take is the Word of God.

The Bible is a Book of principles
as well as a Book of promises.

The Bible is a telescope;
don't look at it, look through it.

The Bible is like a compass;
it always points you in the right direction.

The Bible is not only the world's number
one best-seller, but it is also man's best buy.

The Bible is so simple you have to
have others to help you misunderstand it.

The Bread of Life is never stale!

The Bread of Life makes you GROW.

You can only recall those scriptures
you place in your memory.    18 JAN 2015

You're the only Bible some people ever read.

# BILLBOARDS

Big bang theory? You've got to be kidding.—God

Come on over and bring the kids.—God

Do you have any idea where you are going?—God

Don't make Me come down there.—God

Follow Me.—God

Have you read My number one best-seller?
There will be a test.—God

I love you and you and you and you and. . . . —God

If you're heading in the wrong direction,
God allows U-turns.

Keep using My name in vain, and I'll
make rush hour longer.—God

Let's meet at My house Sunday
before the game.—God

Loved the wedding; invite Me
to the marriage.—God

My way is the high way.—God

Need directions?—God

That "Love thy neighbor" thing . . . I meant it.—God

We need to talk.—God

Billboards

What part of "Thou shalt not . . ."
didn't you understand?—God

Will the road you're on get you to my place?—God

You think it's hot here?—God

# CHANGE AND PROGRESS

Adopt the pace of God.

Be a turtle: he makes progress
when he sticks his neck out.

Better to be pruned than cut up to burn.

Blessed are the flexible, for they
shall not be bent out of shape.

Change is not made without inconvenience.

Change is the watchword of progression.

Conformity is the jailer of freedom
and the enemy of growth.

Every man's destiny is his life preserver.

Everybody is in favor of progress;
it's change they don't like.

Everyone thinks of changing the world,
but no one thinks of changing himself.

Everything changes but change itself.

Goals are like stars; even if not
reached, they can be a guide.

God helps you face the music,
even when you don't like the tune.

He who does not move forward, goes backward.

He who stops changing, ceases growing.

It is a sign of strength to make
changes when necessary.

It's a bad plan that admits of no modification.

Life changes and renews, otherwise it hardens.

Live in the past and go backward; live in the
present and maintain; live in the future and grow.

Misery is a yesterday person trying to
get along with a tomorrow God.

Never forget that only dead fish
swim with the stream.

Nothing dies quicker than a
new idea in a closed mind.

People meet their destiny on the
road they take to avoid it.

"Restlessness and discontent are
the first necessities of progress."—Edison

Some new ideas are just old
ideas with their sleeves rolled up.

The longer a man is in error,
the surer he is that he's right.

The message of the gospel is sacred;
the method by which we share it is not.

The way of progress is neither swift nor easy.

There is nothing as permanent as change.

Things we cannot invent, we can at least improve.

Turn change into opportunity.

We cannot become what we need
to be by remaining what we are.

We must adjust to changing times
by holding to unchanging principles.

When you're through changing, you're through.

Wise people sometimes change
their minds; fools never do.

You can't walk backward into the future.

# CHARACTER

A man has no more character than
he can command in a time of crisis.

A person of words and not of deeds
is like a garden full of weeds.

A person without principle never
draws much interest.

A pint of example is worth a barrel full of advice.

A weak attitude makes weak character.

Ability may get you to the top,
but character will keep you there.

All philosophy lies in two words:
*sustain* and *abstain.*

All virtue is summed up in dealing justly.

An upright man can never be a downright failure.

Be an "amen" Christian, but don't
shout it louder than you live it.

Be what you wish others would be.

Beauty without virtue is a flower without perfume.

Between two evils, choose neither;
between two goods, choose both.

Beware lest your footprints in the sand
of time leave only the marks of a heel.

Beware of no man more than of thyself.

Brains and beauty are God's gifts;
character is your own achievement.

Calamity is a test of integrity.

Character building begins in infancy
and continues until death.

Character builds an existence out of circumstance.

Character is a habit long continued.

Character is developed by two
small words: *yes* and *no.*

Character is easier kept than recovered.

Character is like the foundation of a house—it's
below the surface.

Character is not an inheritance;
each person must build it for himself.

Character is not made in crisis, it is
only exhibited then.

Character is revealed by your actions
in an unguarded moment.

Character is what you are in the dark.

Character is who you are when no
one but God is watching.

Christianity is of no value unless it
changes your character.

Christians aren't perfect, just forgiven.

Christians haven't gone all the way with Christ,
they've just found the right road.

Conquer yourself rather than the world.

Consistent obedience is better
than the occasional sacrifice.

Credibility is believability.

Difficult situations do not make heroes
or cowards, they simply unveil them.

Discipline yourself so others won't have to.

Do you love your weaknesses too
much to defeat them?

Does your walk measure up to your talk?

Don't be a character—have it!

Don't build a case against yourself.

Don't set a bad example while
you're giving good advice.

Don't spend the last half of your
life regretting the first half.

Don't worry about knowing people;
make yourself worth knowing.

Each one sees what is carried in the heart.

Every man is the architect of his own character.

Every man's work is a portrait of himself.

Everyone thinks of changing the world,
but no one thinks of changing himself.

Evil communications corrupt the soul.

Feel far from God?  Who moved?

Few things are more dangerous to
one's character than having nothing to do.

Four cornerstones of character: initiative,
imagination, individuality and independence.

God works from the inside out; Satan
works from the outside in.

Half right is always half wrong.

Have courage to let go of things not worth sticking to.

He is strong who conquers another;
but he who conquers himself is mighty.

He who learns to obey will know how to command.

He who lies down with dogs will rise up with fleas.

He who mistrusts most should be trusted least.

He who would govern others must
first govern himself.

If God is kept outside, something is wrong inside.

If we claim God as our Father, we should act like Him!

If you don't stand for something,
you'll fall for anything.

If you live wrong, you can't die right.

If you pay an ounce of principle for a
pound of popularity, you get badly cheated.

If you want to lead the orchestra, you
must turn your back on the crowd.

Integrity is Christlike character in working clothes.

"It is better to have self-control than to
control an army" (Proverbs 16:32, *TLB*).

It is by acts and not by ideas that people live.

It is not hard to make decisions when
you know what your values are.

It's easier to abstain than refrain.

Jesus obliged us to confess our sins
for our own sake rather than for His.

Knowing what you stand for limits
what you will fall for.

Learn from others' mistakes rather
than making them all yourself.

Live among men as if God were looking;
speak to God as if men were listening.

Live as if you were to die tomorrow.

Live each day so that you are not afraid
of tomorrow nor ashamed of yesterday.

Live so that when people speak evil of you,
no one will believe them.

Live so that you wouldn't be ashamed to
sell the family parrot to the town gossip.

Men's maxims reveal their character.

Moderation is proof of character.

Morality, like art, consists of drawing
the line somewhere.

Much is known of a man's character
by what excites his laughter.

"No man ever got lost on a straight   14 DEC 2014
road."—Abraham Lincoln

Noble deeds concealed are most esteemed.

None are more beautiful or
handsome than one with Christ's reflection.

One test of good manners is to be able
to put up with bad ones.

Others will follow your footsteps
moRE ~~quicker~~ than your advice.  18 APR 2015

Our actions are the best interpreters of our thoughts.

Our present choices determine
our permanent character.

People and rivers become crooked
by following the path of least resistance.

People do not lack strength, they lack will.

People who live right never get left.

Personality is what you are with other people;
character is what you are alone.

Practice what you preach.

Reputation is for time; character is for eternity.

Reputation is the other guy's idea of character.

Reputation is what people think of us;
character is what God knows about us.

Strong drink weakens character.

Take care of your character and your
reputation will take care of itself.

Talents are best nurtured in solitude;
character is formed in trials of the world.

The best sermon is a good example.

The character of our children tomorrow is
shaped by what they learn from us today.

The character we build in this world,
we carry into the next.

The closer we are to the Shepherd,
the farther we are from the wolf.

The first victory you must win is victory over yourself.

The life that is unexamined is not worth living.

The life you live day by day is the
religion you truly possess.

The man who walks with God always
knows what direction he is going.

The sign of wisdom is continual cheerfulness.

The test of your character is what it takes to stop you.

The way of man is lawless the way of God is flawless.

There is never a right time to do the wrong thing.

There's no excellence in all the world
that can be separated from right living.

To be a man is to be responsible.

To build good character, be careful of your choices.

To enjoy the sweet by-and-by,
take care of the now-and-now.

Too often we pray for a change in
our circumstances instead of in our character.

Try not to become a man of success;
become a man of virtue.

Until you are sacrificial, you are artificial.

We inherit personality, but we build character.

What is popular is not always right;
what is right is not always popular.

What lies ahead of you is not as
important as what lies within you.

What you are determines what you do.

What you are speaks so loudly others
can't hear what you say.

When you die you leave behind all you have,
but you take with you all you are.

When you do what you please,
does what you do please God?

You are only what you are when no one is looking.

You can preach a better sermon with
your life than with your lips.

You cannot make a crab walk straight.

You don't have to go to church to be good;
but good people want to go to church.

You never disclose your character better
than when you describe another's.

You show your character by what makes you laugh.

You will think and talk like the person
you listen to the most.

Your choices reflect your character.

Your conversation is a mirror of your thoughts.

Your life is what your thoughts make it.

"Your riches won't help you on Judgment Day; only
righteousness counts then" (Proverbs 11:4, *TLB*).

Your strength is seen in what you stand
for; your weakness in what you fall for.

Your talk doesn't talk like your walk walks.

You're the only Bible some people will ever read.

# CONSCIENCE

A bad conscience has a good memory.

A clear conscience is the softest pillow.

A good conscience is a continual feast.

A person without conviction is like a
ship without a rudder.

Beware of no man more than of thyself.

Conscience is the inner voice that tells
you the IRS might audit your return.

Conscience is the still small voice that
makes you feel still smaller.

Keep conscience clear, then never fear.

Many people tune out their conscience
when money starts to talk.

Money talks louder when your conscience is asleep.

There is no pillow so soft as a clear conscience.

True freedom is a clear conscience.

# HONESTY

A lie has no legs to support itself,
it requires other lies.

A true word needs no oath.

Credibility is believability.

He who cheats at play will cheat you anyway.

He who mistrusts most should be trusted least.

"Honesty is its own defense" (Proverbs 12:13, *TLB*).

Honesty is the best policy.

Honesty is the best policy; too bad there
are so few policyholders.

"No legacy is so rich as honesty."
—William Shakespeare

Sin has many tools, but a lie is the
handle that fits them all.

Truth needs no memory.

"Truth stands the test of time but lies
are soon exposed" (Proverbs 12:19, *TLB*).

When you stretch the truth, watch for the snap back.

# REPUTATION

He who loses honor has nothing else to lose.

Reputation is for time; character is for eternity.

Reputation is the other person's idea of character.

Reputation is what people think of us,
character is what God knows about us.

Shame lasts longer than poverty.

Live so that when people speak evil of
you, no one believes them.

Take care of your character and your
reputation will take care of itself.

# CONFLICT

"A soft tongue can break hard bones" (Proverbs 25:15, *TLB*).

A smooth sea never made a skillful mariner.

A useful life can't be entirely peaceful and carefree.

All sunshine makes a desert.

"Any story sounds true until someone tells the other side" (Proverbs 18:17, *TLB*).

Arguments never settle things; prayer changes things.

If you find a path with no obstacles, it probably doesn't lead anywhere.

If you have no conflicts, you likely have no successes.

If you've not been criticized, you've not done anything.

Nothing contributes more to make a man wise than to have always an enemy in his view.

Others are not necessarily against you, they are merely for themselves.

The best defense is an offense.

To avoid conflict, say nothing, do nothing and be nothing.

Turn into stepping-stones the
bricks others throw at you.

You can't live for God and not
have trouble in the world.

You don't get harmony when
everybody sings the same note.

# CONTENTMENT AND ENVY

A happy heart is better than a full purse.

Abundance, like want, ruins man.

All the world lives in two tents—
content and discontent.

An easy way to become poor is
to pretend you are rich.

Biggest lie ever told: "When I get
what I want, I will be happy."

Contentment is not getting what we want,
but being satisfied with what we have.

Desire nothing for yourself that you
do not desire for others.

Dollars do best when
accompanied by some sense.

Don't grumble if you don't have all you want;
be thankful you don't get what you deserve.

Envy is the desire to have everybody
else a little less successful than you.

Envy provides the mud that
failures throw at success.

Every new possession loads us
with more responsibility.

God always gives His best to those
who leave the choice with Him.

God has already given you what you
need to begin to create your future.

God wants to make us what we need
to be more than give us what we want to have.

God's best gifts are not things but opportunities.

Happiness is a habit to be cultivated.

Happiness is always an inside job.

Happiness is being a child of God.

"Happy are the people whose God is the Lord"
(Psalm 144:15, *NKJV*).

Happy people don't always have the best of
things, but they make the best of thing.

He never promised an easy passage,
only a safe landing.

He who covets is always poor.

He who is content can never be ruined.

If the grass looks greener on the other side,
the water bill is probably higher.

If you don't enjoy what you have,
you won't be happier with more.

If you're green with envy, you're ripe for problems.

It isn't your position that makes you
happy but your disposition.

Joy is spiritual prosperity.

Life is tragic for the person who has
plenty to live on but nothing to live for.

Living above the circumstance is not by chance.

Living for Christ never gets easier,
but it does get better and better.

Love looks through a telescope,
envy through a microscope.

Make the best of it when you get the worst of it.

Make the most of all that comes
and the least of all that goes.

Most of us want what we don't need
and need what we don't want.

Most people would be satisfied with
enough if other people didn't have more.

People always overstate the importance
of things they don't have.

Prayer is not a way to get what we want,
but to become what God wants us to be.

Reality seldom takes into account
your personal preference.

Some Christians are like kittens—only
content when petted.

Start with what you have, not with
what you don't have.

The art of being wise is knowing what to overlook.

The best things in life aren't things.

The grass may be greener on the other
side, but it still must be mowed!

The sign of maturity is accepting
deferred gratification.

The thirst of the soul will never be
quenched by the material things of life.

The unwise person seeks happiness in the future;
the wise person grows it today.

Think of yesterday with pride and tomorrow
with hope to live peacefully today.

We can't always change our circumstances,
but we can change our attitude toward them.

We see things not the way they are,
but the way we are.

When God shuts the door, don't try to
get in through the window.

Who is rich?  Only those who are content.

"Your riches won't help you on Judgment Day; only
righteousness counts then" (Proverbs 11:4, *TLB*).

# CRITICIZING

A critic is a man who knows the way,
but can't drive the car.

A life of complaining is the ultimate rut.

A man's conversation is the mirror of his thoughts.

A pessimist absorbs sunshine and radiates gloom.

A pessimist always complains about the
noise when opportunity knocks.

A pessimist burns his bridges
before he gets to them.

A pessimist can hardly wait for the
future so he can look back with regret.

A pessimist feels bad when he feels good
for fear he'll feel worse if he feels better.

A pint of example is worth a barrel full of advise.

A radical is anyone whose opinion
is different from yours.

A successful man builds with the
bricks others throw at him.

A wise man thinks all he says;
a fool says all he thinks.

A word of advice: don't give any.

Advice is seldom welcome, and those who
want it the most always like it the least.

An obstinate man does not hold
opinions, they hold him.

Any fool can criticize, condemn and
complain, and most fools do.

Blame yourself as you would blame others;
excuse others as you would excuse yourself.

Blessed are the flexible, for they shall
not be bent out of shape.

Criticism is most effective when it sounds like praise.

Criticizing another's garden doesn't
keep the weeds out of your own.

Don't be a cloud just because you can't be a star.

Don't find fault, find a remedy.

Don't grumble if you don't have what you want;
be glad you don't get what you deserve.

Don't point a finger, lend a hand.

Don't spend your life standing
at the complaint counter.

Don't worry about the speck in your friend's eye;
get the plank out of your own.

Each one sees what he carries in his heart.

Envy provides the mud that failures throw at success.

Everyone thinks of changing the world,
but no one thinks of changing himself.

Fear of criticism is the kiss of death
in the courtship of achievement.

Find the good in everyone.

God called us to play the game, not to keep score.

God works from the inside out;
Satan works from the outside in.

Growl all day and you'll feel dog-tired at night.

"He that is without sin . . . let him first
cast a stone" (John 8:7).

He who builds to every man's advice
will have a crooked house.

He who has a heart to help, has a right to criticize.

He who plants thorns must never
expect to gather roses.

He who throws dirt loses ground.

If it were not for doers, the critics
would be out of business.

If there is a hypocrite between you and church,
he is closer to God than you are.

If you are afraid of criticism, you'll die doing nothing.

If you have no critics, you likely have no successes.

If you laid all of man's opinions
end to end, there would be no end.

If your head rises above the crowd,
expect more stones to be thrown at you.

Ignorance is always eager to speak.

Imagination makes a man think he can run
things better than the boss.

Instead of crying over spilled milk,
go milk another cow.

Instead of putting others in their place,
try putting yourself in their place.

Invest time in improving yourself
instead of disapproving in others.

It is much easier to be critical than to be correct.

It isn't your position that makes you happy,
it is your disposition.

It's better to help others get on
than telling them where to get off.

It's better to light a candle than curse the darkness.

It's just as easy to look for the good
things in life as the bad.

It's when the fish opens his
mouth that he gets caught.

Jump to conclusions and suffer from confusion.

Just think about how happy you'd be if you lost
everything you have today and got it back tomorrow.

Let thy discontents be thy secrets.

"Death and life are in the power of the tongue"
(Proverbs 18:21).

Live your life as an exclamation, not an explanation!

Love looks through a telescope,
envy through a microscope.

Many complain of their memory,
but few complain of their judgment.

Many people want to serve God,
but only in an advisory capacity.

Misery wants company.

Most people have too many opinions
and not enough convictions.

No one wants advice—only corroboration.

One man does not see everything.

Our life is what our thoughts make it.

"Out of the abundance of the heart the mouth
speaketh" (Matthew 12:34).

People don't get weak eyes from
looking on the bright side.

Poise is the difference between flipping your
lid and raising your eyebrow.

Satan always attacks those who
can hurt him the most.

Small minds are the first to condemn great ideas.

Small mounds of dirt add up to a mountain.

Small things bother small minds.

Some people approach every
problem with an open mouth.

Some people seem to know how
to live everybody's lives but their own.

Spend your time improving
yourself instead of criticizing others.

The art of being wise is knowing what to overlook.

The best measure of our mentality is the importance of the things we complain about.

The best way to stop stepping on people's toes is to put yourself in their shoes.

The empty vessel makes the greatest sound.

The hardest thing for a person to keep is his opinion.

The loudest boos always come from those in the free seats.

The more you complain, the less you'll obtain.

The person always finding fault seldom finds anything else.

The squeaking wheel doesn't always get the grease; sometimes it gets replaced.

The trouble with ignorance is that it picks up confidence as it goes along.

"The wicked accuse; the godly defend" (Proverbs 12:6, *TLB*).

The worst pest in the world is a pessimist.

There are enough targets to aim at without firing at each other.

There is nothing we receive with so much reluctance as advice.

They who can, DO; those who can't, CRITICIZE.

Think, then speak.

Those who complain about the way the ball bounces, often drop it.

Time and words can never be recalled.

To avoid criticism, say nothing,
do nothing and be nothing.

To belittle is to be little.

To speak kindly does not hurt the tongue.

Trouble is usually produced by
those who produce nothing else.

Tunnel vision tells you
nobody is working as hard as you are.

Unless you are willing to help, don't criticize.

Wanted: Christians who overlook the faults of others
as easily as they do their own.

We cannot always change circumstances,
but we can change our attitude toward them.

We judge ourselves by our motives
and others by their actions.

We may not always agree with God,
but He is still the Boss.

We see things not the way they are,
but the way we are.

When criticizing others, don't forget yourself.

You can always tell failures
by the way they criticize success.

You can tell more about a person by what he says
about others, not what others say about him.

# DREAMS AND IMAGINATION

A goal is a dream without a deadline.

A good idea is like sitting on a tack; it makes you jump up and do something.

Any act of disobedience lengthens the distance between you and your dreams.

Don't try to grow an oak tree in a flowerpot.

Everything great started as somebody's daydream.

Few dreams come true by themselves.

Have old memories and young hopes.

Imagination is more important than knowledge.

Most people never run far enough on their first wind to find out they've got a second.

Never receive counsel from unproductive people.

Opposition, distraction and challenges always surround the birth of a dream.

Pep without purpose is piffle.

Reality is the cage of those who lack imagination.

Small minds are the first to condemn great ideas.

Some people find life an empty dream because they put nothing into it.

The future belongs to those who dream.

The "Man of the Hour" spent many
days and nights getting there.

The person with big dreams is more powerful
than the person with all the facts.

The world would stop if it were run by
those who say, "It can't be done."

There is nothing like a dream to create the future.

To accomplish great things,
we must dream as well as act.

Without a dream you will never realize any high
hope or undertake any high enterprise.

Words without actions are the assassins of dreams.

You cannot depend on your eyes when
your vision is out of focus.

Your dreams are an indicator of
your potential greatness.

Your friends will either stretch your
vision or choke your dreams.

# ENCOURAGEMENT

A diamond is a chunk of coal
that made good under pressure.

A quitter never wins; a winner never quits.

A smooth sea never made a skillful mariner.

A useful life can't be entirely
peaceful and carefree.

Adventures begin when we dare
to do the impossible with God.

All sunshine makes a desert.

All the world lives in two tents—content
and discontent.

Always laugh when you can—it
is cheap medicine.

Anyone can hold the helm when the sea is calm.

Anyone who has never made a mistake
has never tried anything new.

Be like the tea kettle—sing when you're
in hot water up to your nose.

Be still and know that He is God.

Christianity helps us face the music
even if we don't like the tune.

74

Christians aren't perfect . . . just forgiven.

Clear your mind of "can't."

Correction does much; encouragement does more.

Courage is resistance of fear, not absence of fear.

Don't be afraid to go out on a limb;
that's where the fruit is.

Don't be discouraged by failure
or satisfied with success.

Don't let what you cannot do
interfere with what you can.

Dry spells cause roots to go deep.

Each of us matters to God.

Earth hath no sorrow that heaven cannot heal.

Encouragement is oxygen to the soul.

Even perfect people buy pencils with erasers.

Even the biggest dog was once a pup.

Even the lion has to defend himself against gnats.

Even the sun has a sinking spell every night,
but it rises again in the morning.

Every day holds the possibility of miracles.

Every great achievement was once impossible.

Every new adjustment is a crisis in self-esteem.

Everything is difficult before it is easy.

Experience is what you get while
you are looking for something else.

Face the music and someday you will lead the band.

Face the sunshine and the shadows will fall behind.

Failure is never final.

Failure is never permanent.

Failure is only a detour on the road to success.

*03 DEC 2014* God doesn't call the qualified; He qualifies the called.

God gives us the abilities to soar beyond our
problems to our possibilities.

God is in control.

God keeps His promises.

God knew what He was doing when He made you.

God likes surprises. Breaking a mold is His specialty.

God makes no junk.

God may break us in order to remake us.

God never said the road would be easy,
but He did promise you'd never be alone.

God plus one is always a majority.

God sometimes moves mountains
one pebble at a time.

God's love has been tried and found true.

God's resources are always
equal to His requirements.

God's timing is always perfect.

Grow where you are planted.

Happy people don't always have the best of things,
but they make the best of everything.

He knows you and He loves you!

He never promised an easy passage,
only a safe landing.

He that stays in the valley shall never get over the hill.

Honey is sweet, but the bee stings.

HOPE: He Offers Peace Eternal.

Hope for the best, expect the worst,
and enjoy the in-between.

Hope is a good anchor,
but it needs something to grip.

Hope lives in the heart of the believer.

I can call on Jesus anytime—He
is always on the line.

I put my trust in the Lord's hand
so I might understand.

If it's raining in your life, pop up the
umbrella of God's protection.

If the going is getting easier, you aren't climbing.

If the going is real easy, be careful
you aren't going downhill.

If the grass looks greener on the other side of the
fence, the water bill is probably higher.

If there is no wind, row.

If you can't see the bright side, polish the dull side.

If you continue to do what's right,
what's wrong will leave your life.

If you find a path with no obstacles,
it probably doesn't lead anywhere.

If you have no critics, you likely have no successes.

If you know God, you will trust Him.

If you want a place in the sun,
you've got to expect a few blisters.

If you want the rainbow, you gotta
put up with the rain.

If you've not been criticized,
you've not done anything.

In the middle of difficulty lies opportunity.

In trying times, don't quit trying.

Instead of crying over spilled milk,
go milk another cow.

Into each life some rain must fall.

It's courage that counts.

It's looking down that makes one dizzy.

It's not how far you fall but how high
you bounce that makes the difference.

Jesus cares.

Jesus is a friend who walks in when
the world has walked out.

Jesus is the Rock and He can roll your blues away.

Jesus never fails.

Jesus: our hope for today, our hope for tomorrow.

Keep your face to the sunshine and
you cannot see the shadow.

Laughing helps; it's like jogging on the inside.

Life's disappointments are opportunity's
hidden appointments.

Life's not fair, but God is faithful.

Living above the circumstance Is not by chance!

Living for Christ never gets easier,
but it does get better and better.

Long-range goals keep you from getting
discouraged with short-term failure.

Make the best of it when you get the worst of it.

Most successes are built on failures.

No matter what your past has been,
your future is spotless.

Not to have tried is the true failure.

Obstacles are those things you see when
you take your eyes off God.

Obstacles are what you see when you
take your eyes off the goal.

On the streets of by-and-by, one arrives
at the house of "never."

One, on God's side, is a majority.

Only those who dare to fail greatly
can ever achieve greatly.

People are like tea bags—you have to put
them in hot water to know how strong they are.

Pressure turns a lump of coal into a diamond.

Put God in the center and
everything will come together.

Remember, the mighty oak tree
was once a little nut.

Satan always attacks those
who can hurt him the most.

Sometimes changing yourself changes everything.

Step by step, prayer by prayer,
God will always get you there.

Success doesn't eliminate obstacles,
it creates new ones.

The best defense is an offense.

The best way to forget your problem is
to help someone solve theirs.

The Burden Bearer is our Carrier.

The devil wants you to think that your
temporary situation is permanent.

The greater the difficulty, the greater the glory.

The harder you fall, the higher you bounce!

The only difference between stumbling blocks and
stepping-stones is how you use them.

The storm also beats on the house
that's built on the Rock.

The task ahead of you is never as
great as the power behind you.

The thickest clouds often bring the
heaviest shower of blessing.

The whole ocean is made up of little drops.

There are no unimportant people.

There can be no rainbow without a cloud or a storm.

There is a place for people with no problems;
it's called the cemetery.

There is no fruit that is not bitter before it is ripe.

There is no road too hard when we walk by His side.

Things look up when you look to God.

To avoid criticism say nothing,
do nothing, and be nothing.

To every disadvantage there is
a corresponding advantage.

To lose is to learn.

Today is not won by old victories,
nor lost by old defeats.

Too many people miss the silver lining
because they're expecting gold.

Trouble is only opportunity in work clothes.

Turn into stepping-stones the
bricks others throw at you.

We are all precious in His sight.

We can't always change circumstances,
but we can change our attitude toward them.

We lose a lot of battles in the
process of winning the war.

What is worthwhile is always difficult.

Whatever is good to know is difficult to learn.

When down in the mouth, remember
Jonah; he came out all right.

When it's dark enough, you can see the stars.

When Satan brings up your past, bring up his future.

When there is pruning, the Gardener is nearby.

When we do what we can, God will do what we can't.

When we pray for rain, we must be
willing to put up with a little mud.

When you come to a roadblock, take a detour.

You can get out of God's will, but
never out of His reach.

You can't live for God and not have
trouble in the world.

You don't need to know the how's and
why's when you know the Who.

You have been given the seeds for greatness.

You haven't failed until you quit trying.

You were created to be an answer.

You're like a tea bag, not worth much
till you've been through some hot water.

# FAILURE AND MISTAKES

A life spent making mistakes is more
useful than a life spent doing nothing.

A man's errors are what make him amiable.

An upright man can never be a downright failure.

Excuses are the nails used to
build a house of failure.

Failure is not a crime; failure to attempt is.

It is hard to fail, but it is worse never
to have tried to succeed.

It's not whether you failed, but whether
you are content with your failure.

Mistakes are the portals of discovery.

Most successes are built on failures.

Only those who dare to fail greatly
can ever achieve greatly.

Success comes in "cans"; failure
comes in "cant's."

The greatest mistake is to continually
fear you will make one.

The train of failure usually runs
on the track of laziness.

The worst failure is failure to try.

You always pass failure on the way to success.

You can always tell a failure by the
way he criticizes success.

You learn more from mistakes than from successes.

# FAITH

Adventures begin when we dare
to do the impossible with God.

An atheist is a man who has no
invisible means of support.

Are you standing on God's promises
or just sitting on the premises?

Are you waiting on God, or is He waiting on you?

Believe you can, and you're halfway there.
Believe God can, and the race is won.

Don't be afraid to go out on a limb—that's
where the fruit is.

Don't pray for a bushel and only carry a cup.

Doubt builds a mountain; faith moves it. 04 JAN 2015

Every day holds the possibility of miracles.

Fact:  God is.    9/28/2014

Faith demands a decision before it can work.

Faith enables us to withstand
what we can't understand.

Faith focuses on God instead of the problem.

Faith is holding on to God's dreams
and finding your own fulfilled.

Faith is like driving in the fog.

Faith is not belief without proof
but trust without reservation.

Faith is the capacity to endure uncertainty.

Faith isn't a leap in the dark but a step into the light.

Faith keeps the person who keeps the faith.

Faith must span the chasm of sense and time.

Faith to move mountains comes
from the living fountain.

"Faith without works is dead" (James 2:26).

Fear immobilizes, faith empowers.

Feed your faith and your doubts will starve to death.

God plus one is always a majority.

God uses the insignificant to
accomplish the impossible.

God's resources are always
equal to His requirements.

God's timing is always perfect.

Have your faith lifted here!

He that stays in the valley shall never get over the hill.

He who expects nothing shall never be disappointed.

He's an "on time" God.

I can call on Jesus anytime—He is always on the line.

I put my trust in the Lord's hand
so I might understand.

If you know God, you will trust Him.

It's just as easy to look for the
good things in life as the bad.

Need some color in your life?

Give Jesus the paintbrush.

Never put a question mark where God put a period.

Paul never said, "I know what I believe,"
but "I know whom I believe."

Prayer is asking for rain; faith is
carrying the umbrella.

Prayer need not be long when faith is strong.

Small matches light great torches.

Sorrow looks back, worry looks
around, but faith looks up.

"The just shall live by faith" (Romans 1:17).

The trouble with atheism is that it has no future.

They are able who think they are able.

Walk by faith, not by feelings.

We need the root to bear fruit.

"We walk by faith, not by sight" (2 Corinthians 5:7).

When faith is stretched, it grows.

When the outlook is bad, try the up-look.

When we tap into God's eternal power,
our resources are limitless.

"Without faith it is impossible to please Him"
(Hebrews 11:6, NKJV).

You do not find what you do not seek.

# FEAR, WORRY AND COURAGE

A great deal of talent is lost for
want of a little courage.

All our fret and worry is caused
by calculating without God.

Anything worth worrying about
is worth praying about.

As long as God's direction is your
friend, don't worry about your enemies.

Courage is fear holding on a minute longer.

Courage is fear that has said its prayers.

Courage is grace under power.

Courage is mastery of fear, not absence of fear.

Courage is the quality that guarantees all others.

Do the thing you fear and the
death of fear is certain.

Fear immobilizes, faith empowers.

"Fear not: for I am with thee" (Isaiah 43:5).

Fear of criticism is the kiss of
death in the courtship of achievement.

Fear wants you to run from
something that isn't after you.

Feed your faith and your fears will starve to death.

Give your worries to God; He will be
up all night anyway.

God doesn't want to beat you up,
He wants to build you up.

Greet the unseen with cheer, not fear.

He never promised an easy
passage, only a safe landing.

He who builds to every man's advice
will have a crooked house.

I can call on Jesus anytime; He is always on the line.

If all men you must please, you will never be at ease.

If you know God, you will trust Him.

If you want today's fire to burn brightly,
throw out yesterday's ashes.

It is better to try something and
fail than try nothing and succeed.

Jesus, our hope for today, our hope for tomorrow.

Jump to conclusions and suffer from confusion.

Keep conscience clear, then never fear.

Life shrinks and expands
in proportion to one's courage.

Most people look too far ahead for things close by.

Necessity does the work of courage.

Never put a question mark
where God has put a period.    24mar 2015

No God, no peace . . . Know God, know peace.

"No weapon formed against you shall prosper"
(Isaiah 54:17, *NKJV*).

Nothing will ever be attempted if all
possible objections must first be overcome.

Obstacles are those things you see
when you take your eyes off God.

Only God knows what's beyond the
horizon; leave it in His hands.

Our doubts are traitors—they make us lose
the good we might win by fearing to attempt.

Procrastination is the symptom; fear is the problem.

Real peace is knowing the God who
holds your future in His hands.

The rewards of the journey far
outweigh the risk of leaving the harbor.

The unknown holds no fear for those who follow God.

There are 365 "Fear Nots" in the
Bible—one for each day!

There is no such thing as bravery,
just degrees of fear.

We see things not the way they
are, but the way we are.

Why worry when you can pray?

Worry is like a rocking chair; no matter
how long you rock, you get nowhere.

Worry is the first sign of unbelief.

Worry is the interest paid by those
who borrow trouble.

Worry is the interest paid on trouble
before it becomes due.

Worry is the misuse of imagination.

Worry is tomorrow's mouse eating today's cheese.

Yesterday is past, tomorrow may never
come. We have only today.

You cannot discover new oceans unless you
have the courage to lose sight of the shore.

You have the rest of your life to be
miserable, so enjoy today!

# FORGIVENESS AND REVENGE

A chip on the shoulder indicates
there is wood higher up.

A forgiving spirit opens the way to better things.

An argument is the longest
distance between two points.

Christians are not perfect, just forgiven.

"Do not repay anyone evil for evil"
(Romans 12:17, *NIV*).

"Forgive, and ye shall be forgiven" (Luke 6:37).

Forgive your enemies—nothing annoys them more.

Forgiveness is an attribute of the strong.

The weak never forgive.

Forgiveness is not an occasional
act but a permanent attitude.

Forgiveness means giving
up your rights to revenge.

Getting even with someone
means putting yourself on their level.

He who cannot forgive destroys a bridge
he may someday need to pass.

If you want today's fire to burn brightly,
throw out yesterday's ashes.

Learn to lean on others strengths
and forgive their weaknesses.

Love is blind, friendship closes its eyes.

Malice hath a strong memory.

Never cut what can be untied.

Patting someone on the back is the
best way to get a chip off the shoulder.

Revenge proves its own executioner.

The best way to get the last word is to apologize.

The surest way to get rid of an enemy
is to make a friend of him.

There is no revenge so sweet as forgiveness.

Time and words can never be recalled.

To forget a wrong is the best revenge.

Unforgiveness has no foresight.

Unless we forgive, we destroy the bridge
by which God is able to forgive us.

We judge ourselves by our motives
and others by their actions.

While you're carrying the weight of a grudge,
the other guy is out producing.

You can't get ahead when you are trying to get even.

# FRIENDSHIP

A friend in need is a friend indeed.

A friend is a present you give yourself.

A friend is never known until he is needed.

A person with a lot of friends either
has a lot of money or is a good listener.

A true friend is the greatest of all blessings.

Choose friends who pull you up,
not drag you down.

Don't ever slam the door;
you might want to go back.

Don't worry about knowing people;
make yourself worth knowing.

Few burdens are heavy when everybody lifts.

Friends are like buttons on an elevator; they will
take you up or they will take you down.

Friends ask how you are and
then wait for the answer.

Friendship is a sheltering tree.

Friendship is like a bank account; you can't
continue to draw on it without making deposits.

God gave you two ears and one mouth.
Are you listening?

"Gossip separates the best of friends"
(Proverbs 16:28, *TLB*).

Hatred watches while friendship sleeps.

He makes no friend who never made a foe.

He who lies down with dogs will rise up with fleas.

Hear much, speak little.

If you win all your arguments,
you'll end up with no friends.

In prosperity friends know us;
in adversity we know our friends.

It's not the difference between people
that is the difficulty; it's the indifference.

Jesus is a friend who walks in
when the world has walked out.

Leadership is a relationship.

Leave everyone a little better than you found them.

Love is blind, friendship closes its eyes.

Most smiles are started by another smile.

No one has so big a house that he
does not need a good neighbor.

No one makes it alone.

No one person alone can match
the efforts of a united team.

None knows the weight of another one's burden.

Openness is to wholeness as
secrets are to sickness.

People don't care how much you know
until they know how much you care.

Prosperity makes friends, adversity tries them.

Short visits make long friends.

Talking is sharing, but listening is caring.

The best antique is an old friend.

The best vitamin for making friends: B1.

The best way to stop stepping on people's toes
is to put yourself in their shoes.

The company you keep will determine
the trouble you meet.

The fence that shuts others out shuts you in.

The greatest ability in life is to get along with others.

The ornaments of a house are
the friends who frequent it.

The surest way to get rid of an enemy
is to make a friend of him.

To have a friend, you must be a friend.

Treat your friends like your pictures
and place them in their best light.

We need to love people and use things
instead of using people and loving things.

Weak things united become strong.

You cannot shake hands with a clenched fist.

Your friends will stretch your vision
or choke your dreams.

# GIVING

A rejected opportunity to give is a
lost opportunity to receive.

A small gift is better than a great promise.

By watering others, you water yourself.

Christians show what they are by what
they do with what they have.

God sees what we give and what we withhold.

God will never ask you for something
you can't give Him.

He who lends to the poor gets interest from God.

How many happy selfish people do you know?

Invest in the success of others.

"It is more blessed to give than to receive"
(Acts 20:35).

"It is possible to give away and become richer!"
(Proverbs 11:24, *TLB*).

It is possible to hold on too tightly
and lose everything.

It's not the difference between people that is
the difficulty; it's the indifference.

It's not what we get, but what we give,
that makes us rich.

Leave everyone a little better than you found them.

No man is more deceived than the selfish man.

No person is ever honored for what he received.
Honor is a reward for what he gave.

Real generosity is doing something nice
for someone who'll never know the giver.

The closer you are to God, the less important
are worldly pleasures and treasures.

The Dead Sea is dead because
it only receives and never gives.

We make a living by what we get;
we make a life by what we give.

What matters most in life is
what you have done for others.

"Whatsoever good thing any man doeth, the same
shall he receive" (Ephesians 6:8).

You grow spiritually to the extent that you give out.

# GOSSIP

Gossipers always gets caught in
their own mouth-trap.

A gossip is a newscaster without the sponsor.

A gossip is like old shoes—
tongues never stay in place.

A man never discloses his character more
clearly as when he describes another's.

A person who knows everything
has the most to learn.

A shut mouth catches no flies.

A shut mouth gathers no foot.

A wise man thinks all he says;
a fool says all he thinks.

All cruelty springs from weakness.

An idle mind is the devil's workshop.

"Any story sounds true until someone
tells the other side and sets the record
straight" (Proverbs 18:17, *TLB*).

Empty barrels make the most noise.

Ever wonder why God gave us
two ears and one mouth?

Everybody's business is nobody's business.

Expect poison from standing water.

Faultfinding is like window washing—all the dirt seems to be on the other side.

Give less advice and more of a hand.

Gossip is like mud on the wall; you can wipe it off, but it leaves a mark.

Gossip is the art of saying nothing in a way that leaves nothing unsaid.

Gossip runs down more people than automobiles.

"Gossip separates the best of friends" (Proverbs 16:28, *TLB*).

Half the evil in the world is gossip started by good people.

He hears but half who hears only one party.

He that blows the fire will get sparks in his eyes.

He who pries into every cloud may be stricken with a thunderbolt.

He who throws dirt loses ground.

Hear much, speak little.

Honesty is the best policy.

If you cannot be a runner-up, try not to be a runner-down.

It's just as easy to look for the good things in life as the bad.

Keeping a secret is like trying to smuggle daylight past a rooster.

Let us keep our mouths shut and our pens
dry until we know all the facts.

Live so that you wouldn't be ashamed to sell
the family parrot to the town gossip.

Mansions in the sky cannot be built
out of mud thrown at others.

None are so busy as those who do nothing.

Nothing will stir up more mud
than a groundless rumor.

Pour water, not gasoline, on fires of gossip.

Rumor is a great traveler.

Silence often does more harm to truth than do lies.

Small matches light great torches.

Speech is silver, silence is golden.

Spend your time improving yourself
instead of criticizing others.

The best way to avoid a nose bleed is
to stay out of other people's business.

The difference between gossip and news
is whether you hear it or tell it.

The eyes believe themselves,
the ears believe other people.

"The first to present his case seems right,
till another comes forward and questions him"
(Proverbs 18:17, *NIV*).

The less men think, the more they talk.

The loudest boos always come
from those in the free seats.

"The wicked accuse; the godly defend"
(Proverbs12:6, *TLB*).

Think, then speak.

Throwing mud makes you dirty.

Time and words can never be recalled.

To belittle is to be little.

Trouble is usually produced by
those who produce nothing else.

"Truth stands the test of time, but lies are soon
exposed" (Proverbs 12:19, *TLB*).

Two things are bad for the heart—running
upstairs and running down people.

Wanted: people who overlook the faults of
others as easily as they do their own.

We judge ourselves by our motives
and others by their actions.

What some invent, the rest enlarge.

When criticizing others, don't forget yourself.

When hearing gossip, we should
not file or copy it, but shred it.

Where the river is deepest, it makes the least noise.

Whoever gossips to you will gossip about you.

Why do people who know
the least know it the loudest?

Words spoken can never be recalled.

Work with the construction gang,
not the wrecking crew.

You are the master of the unspoken word
but the slave of the words spoken.

You can make a mountain out of a molehill
by adding a little dirt.

You can't act like a skunk without
someone getting wind of it.

You can't be hurt by something you didn't say.

You never disclose your character more clearly
than when you describe another's.

You never see a fish on the wall with its mouth shut.

Your ears aren't made to shut, but your mouth is.

# HABITS

A habit never goes away by itself.

A nail is driven out by another nail;
habit is overcome by habit.

All philosophy lies in two words:
*sustain* and *abstain*.

Character is a habit long continued.

Conquer yourself rather than the world.

Defending your faults proves you
have no intention of quitting them.

Do you love your weaknesses too
much to defeat them?

Don't be discouraged by failure
or satisfied with success.

Drinking is committing suicide
on the installment plan.

God sometimes moves mountains
one pebble at a time.

Good habits result from resisting temptation.

Habit, if not resisted, soon becomes a necessity.

Habits are first cobwebs, then cables.

Habits must be coaxed down a step at a time.

Have courage to let go of things not worth sticking to.

He is strong who conquers another;
but he who conquers himself is mighty.

If you continue to do what's right,
what's wrong will leave your life.

It's easier to abstain than refrain.

It's easier to prevent bad habits than to break them.

Laws are never as effective as habits.

Moderation is proof of character.

Nothing needs reforming as much
as other people's habits.

Nothing will ever be attempted if all
possible objections must first be overcome.

People do not lack strength, they lack will.

Small matches light great torches.

Some remedies are worse than the disease.

The beginning of health is to know the disease.

The best throw of the dice is to throw them away.

The best way to squeeze out a bad
habit is to replace it with a good one.

The chains of habit are too weak to
be felt until they are too strong to be broken.

The first victory you must win is over yourself.

The man who drinks much thinks little.

The more you pour out, the more God pours in.

The nature of men is always the same;
it is their habits that separate them.

There is no such thing as great talent
without great willpower.

Today is not won by old victories
nor lost by old defeats.

Watch your actions—they become habits.

We first make our habits, and then
our habits make us.

Why are good habits easier to
give up than bad ones?

You will think and talk like the person
you listen to the most.

# HOLIDAYS

## NEW YEAR'S DAY

God can make all things new, even you.

Let your resolution be God's solution.

No matter what your past, your future is spotless.

## VALENTINE'S DAY

A happy marriage to another requires
a divorce from yourself.

God can heal a broken heart,
but He has to have all the pieces.

God is love.

God's love has been tried and found true.

"Hatred stirreth up strifes; but love
covereth all sins" (Proverbs 10:12).

I love you and you and you and you and. . . . —God

Love and respect.  You can't have a
healthy relationship without either one.

Love doesn't dominate; it cultivates.

Love doesn't keep score.

Love is a language everyone understands.

Love is blind, and marriage is the eye-opener.

Love is blind, friendship closes its eyes.

Love is the medicine for the sickness of the world.

Love one another.

Love sees through a telescope, not a microscope.

# EASTER

Christ crossed out our sin on Calvary.

Christ is Life, the rest is details.

Easter—the rest of the Christmas story.

"God so loved the world that he gave his only begotten Son" (John 3:16).

GRACE: God's Riches At Christ's Expense.

Hallelujah! Jesus is alive!

His pain—our gain.

Jesus burst from the grave and exploded in our hearts.

Jesus rose from the dead. You can get up out of the bed on Easter Sunday, 10 a.m.

Nails could not have kept Jesus on the cross had not love held Him there.

One person CAN make a difference. Jesus did!

Salvation is free, because Jesus paid the price.

The Cross is the last argument of God.

The Cross is the only ladder tall enough
to reach heaven.

# MOTHER'S DAY

"A foolish man despises his mother"
(Proverbs 15:20, *NKJV*).

An ounce of mother is worth more
than a pound of clergy.

Home is wherever Mom is.

"Honor your father and your mother"
(Exodus 20:12, *NKJV*).

Nobody is poor who has had a godly mother.

Remember when we honored father and
mother instead of all the major credit cards?

The best gift a father can give his children
is to love their mother.

# FATHER'S DAY

A father is someone you look up to no
matter how tall you grow.

A man without principle never draws much interest.

An upright man can never be a downright failure.

Good fathers don't just give life,
they teach how to live.

"Listen to a father's instruction . . . and gain
understanding" (Proverbs 4:1, *NIV*).

Thank God for fathers who not only gave us life
but also taught us how to live.

The best inheritance a father can
leave is a good example.

"The steps of a good man are ordered by the Lord"
(Psalm 37:23).

The trouble with parenting is that by the time
we're experienced, we're unemployed.

Try not to become a man of success,
but a man of virtue.

# INDEPENDENCE DAY

A nation is only as good as the people in it.

A nation is only as strong as the
character of its people.

A nation without conviction is like a
ship without a rudder.

A people that values its privileges
over its principles soon loses both.

"Blessed is the nation whose God is the Lord"
(Psalm 33:12).

God bless the U.S.A.

God knows our history and our future.

"Godliness exalts a nation, but sin is a reproach
to any people" (Proverbs 14:34, *TLB*).

"If my people . . . shall humble themselves, and pray . . . I will heal their land" (2 Chronicles 7:14).

"In God We Trust." Right on the money.

No God—no peace. Know God—know peace.

One nation, under God, is indivisible.

"Righteousness exalteth a nation" (Proverbs 14:34).

# THANKSGIVING

A good conscience is a continual feast.

Count your blessings instead of sheep.

Count your blessings, name them one by one.

Don't grumble if you don't have what you want; be glad you don't get what you deserve.

Gratitude is the parent of all other virtues.

Have an attitude of gratitude.

He who is thankful for little enjoys much.

"In everything, give thanks" (1 Thessalonians 5:18).

Ingratitude is the daughter of pride.

Ingratitude is the mother of every vice.

Judge this day not by the harvest but by the seeds planted.

Thankfulness is the soil where joy thrives.

Thanksgiving is thanks living.

There is always something to be thankful for.

Too busy adding up your troubles
to count your blessings?

# CHRISTMAS

Don't leave CHRIST out of CHRISTmas.

Jesus Came to us so we can go to Him.

Jesus is the reason for the season.

Joy to the world, the Lord has come!

O come let us adore Him.

The best Christmas gift was wrapped in a manger.

"Unto you was born this day . . .
a Savior" (Luke 2:11).

Wise men still seek Him today.

# JUST FOR FUN

A chip on the shoulder indicates
there is wood higher up.

A Christian heart is a good thing,
but a Christian liver is much better.

A Christian without a church is like
a bee without a hive.

A full cabin is better than an empty castle.

A gossip always gets caught in
their own mouth-trap.

A gossip is a newscaster without the sponsor.

A man who toots his own horn soon has
everybody dodging when he approaches.

A man wrapped up in himself
makes a very small package.

A mighty oak was once a little
nut that stood his ground!

A pessimist always complains about
the noise when opportunity knocks.

A pessimist burns his bridges
before he gets to them.

A pessimist can hardly wait for the future
so he can look back with regret.

A pessimist feels bad when he feels good
for fear he'll feel worse if he feels better.

A sense of humor is like a needle and thread—it
will patch up many things.

A shut mouth catches no flies.

A shut mouth gathers no foot.

A smile is a little curve that makes things straight.

A wise man gets more use from his
enemies than a fool from his friends.

Age doesn't matter unless you are cheese.

Always laugh when you can—it is cheap medicine.

Always remember—you're unique,
just like everyone else.

An atheist is a man who has no
invisible means of support.

An imperfect person is always
looking for a perfect pastor.

Any plant growing in the wrong place is a weed.

Appearing soon . . . live and in
person . . . Jesus Christ!

As long as there are tests, there will always
be prayer in public schools.

Be like the teakettle—sing when you're in
hot water up to your nose.

Be like the woodpecker: use your
head and keep pecking!

Be open-minded . . . but not so open-minded
your brains fall out.

Better to be patient on the road than
a patient in the hospital.

Beware lest your footprints in the sand of time
leave only the marks of a heel.

Churches belong to the community . . . attend one.

Come in and let us help you prepare for your finals.

Consider yourself hugged.

Do not wait for the hearse to take you to church.

Do you have a backbone or a wishbone?

Don't grumble if you don't have what you want;
be glad you don't get what you deserve.

Don't try to grow an oak tree in a flowerpot.

Don't wail on the scale if you cheat when you eat.

Don't wait till you get to heaven to
start acting like an angel.

Don't wait until you die to be brought to church.

Dusty Bibles lead to dirty lives.

Even a fly doesn't get a slap on the
back until he starts to work.

Even a stopped clock is right twice a day.

Expect poison from standing water.

Experience is the name we give to our mistakes.

Experience is what you get while you are
looking for something else.

Families are like fudge—mostly sweet
with a few nuts.

Faultfinding is like window washing—all the dirt
seems to be on the other side.

Fight truth decay—study the Bible daily.

Floating members make a sinking church.

For a mansion in heaven,
make your reservations now!

Forbidden fruit creates many jams.

Get a life! Live for Christ.

Getting even with others means
putting yourself on their level.

Give Satan an inch and he'll become a ruler.

God—don't leave home without Him.

God is a Promise Keeper.

God never goes on vacation.

God should be our steering wheel, not our spare tire.

God's top ten list . . . the Ten Commandments.

Good resolutions are like babies crying in
church—they should be carried out immediately.

GOOD without GOD becomes 0.

Got Jesus?

Growl all day and you'll feel dog tired at night.

Have your faith lifted here!

He that blows the fire will get sparks in his eyes.

He who buries his talent is making a grave mistake.

He who laughs, lasts.

He who lies down with dogs will rise up with fleas.

He who pries into every cloud may be
stricken with a thunderbolt.

He who throws dirt loses ground.

Heaven: don't miss it for the world!

Heaven goes by favor. If it went by merit, you would
stay out and your dog would go in.

Heaven knows when you were here last!

Horse sense comes from a stable mind.

Humor is gravity concealed behind a jest.

If the grass looks greener on the other side of the
fence, the water bill is probably higher.

If we claim God as our Father,
we should act like Him!

If you burn the candle at both ends
you are not as bright as you think.

If you cannot be a runner-up,
try not to be a runner-down.

If you don't want the fruits of sin,
stay out of the devil's orchard.

If you stand in the middle of the road,
you'll get knocked down by both sides.

If you want a place in the sun,
you've got to expect a few blisters.

If you win all your arguments,
you'll end up with no friends.

If you're looking for a sign from God, this is it!

If you're not going to put your quarter
in the phone, get out of the booth.

If your mind goes blank,
be sure to turn off the sound.

Instead of crying over spilled milk,
go milk another cow.

Ironing out problems without Jesus
puts wrinkles on your face.

It is an ironic habit of human beings
to run faster when we have lost our way.

It is easy to see through people
who make spectacles of themselves.

It wasn't the apple on the tree but the pair beneath.

It's better to be silent and considered a fool
than to open your mouth and remove all doubt.

It's better to help others to get on rather
than telling them where to get off.

It's easy to be an angel if
no one ruffles your feathers.

Jesus is the Rock; is your name on the roll?

Keeping a secret is like trying to smuggle
daylight past a rooster.

Laughter is contagious; start an epidemic!

Let God unravel the tangles in your life.

Life is a puzzle; look here for your missing piece.

Live so that you wouldn't be ashamed to
sell the family parrot to the town gossip.

Living without God means dying without hope.

Love is blind, and marriage is the eye-opener.

Most men forget God all day but ask
Him to remember them at night.

Neglect to drink of the spring of experience
and die of thirst in the desert of ignorance.

Only fools fool with sin.

Pick your friends, but not to pieces.

Planning to go to heaven?
Get your reservations here.

Raising teenagers is like nailing Jell-O to a tree.

Remember, you're an original,
just like everybody else.

Serving God is like learning to play golf—keep your
knees bent and your arms extended.

Smile! God loves you!

Some Christians are like kittens,
only content when petted.

Some food for thought is only baloney.

Some minds are like concrete . . .
thoroughly mixed and permanently set.

Some people attend church three times—when
they're hatched, matched and dispatched.

The banana that leaves the bunch gets peeled.

The loudest boos always come from
those in the free seats.

The person with a small mind
usually has a big mouth.

The recipe for a good speech includes
some shortening.

The right train of thought can take you
to a better station in life.

The trouble with ignorance is that it
picks up confidence as it goes along.

The way to get to the top is to get off your bottom.

The world is full of cactus, but we
don't have to sit on it.

The world's experts made the Titanic;
God's amateurs made the ark.

Those who testify by the yard and live by
the inch ought to be kicked in the foot.

Today is a gift . . . that's why
it's called "the present."

Treat yourself to one of our Sundays!

Try one of our Sundays—they're better
than Baskin Robbins!

We believe in Prophet-Sharing.

What on earth are you doing for Heaven's sake?

What would Jesus do?

What's missing from our CH  CH? U R.

When down in the mouth, remember
Jonah; he came out all right.

When you flee temptations, don't leave
a forwarding address.

When you're a self-starter, others
don't have to be a crank.

Why do some people think they are
exceptions to the rules?

Work with the construction gang,
not the wrecking crew.

Worry is tomorrow's mouse eating today's cheese.

You can make a mountain out of a
molehill by adding a little dirt.

You can send your marriage to the
grave with a series of little digs.

You can't act like a skunk without
someone getting wind of it.

# KINDNESS

A drop of honey catches more
flies than a gallon of gall.

A smile is a little curve that sets things straight.

A smile is an inexpensive way
to improve your face value.

A smile is an inexpensive
way to improve your looks.

A smile is the shortest distance
between two people.

"A soft tongue can break hard bones"
(Proverbs 25:15, *TLB*).

A world in despair needs people who care.

Courtesy costs nothing; but its worth is priceless.

Find the good in everyone.

Forget yourself for others,
and others will not forget you.

Good manners are made up of petty sacrifices.

If you haven't got kindness in your heart, you
have the worst kind of heart trouble.

If you want to be great, be the servant of all.

It's better to be hurt than to cause hurt.

It's not the difference between people that is
the difficulty; it's the indifference.

It's when we forget ourselves that we do
things that are remembered.

JOY: Jesus first, others second, yourself last.

Joy shared is joy doubled.

"Kind words are like honey—enjoyable and healthful"
(Proverbs 16:24, *TLB*).

Kindness consists in loving people
more than they deserve.

Kindness has won more people than
zeal, science or eloquence.

Kindness is to the heart what
sunshine is to the flowers.

Learn to lean on others' strengths
and forgive their weaknesses.

Leave everyone a little better than you found them.

Make yourself indispensable to somebody.

Most smiles are started by another smile.

Nothing costs as little and goes as far as courtesy.

Nothing is as strong as gentleness, and nothing
is as gentle as true strength.

One test of good manners is to be able
to put up with bad ones.

People don't care how much you know
until they know how much you care.

People need love most when
they deserve it the least.

People will treat you the way you view them.

Perhaps the most important trip you will
ever make is going the second mile.

Politeness goes far, yet costs nothing.

Politeness is the art of choosing
among one's real thoughts.

Practice random acts of kindness.

Real generosity is doing something nice
for someone who'll never find it out.

Talking is sharing . . . but listening is caring.

The best way to stop stepping on people's
toes is to put yourself in their shoes.

The really great man is the man who
makes every man feel great.

There is no better exercise than reaching
down and lifting someone up.

Those who bring sunshine to others
cannot keep it from themselves.

To speak kindly does not hurt the tongue.

"Whatsoever good thing any man doeth,
the same shall he receive" (Ephesians 6:8).

You never get a second chance
to make a good first impression.

Your heart has eyes the brain knows nothing of.

# LAZINESS

A person of words and not of deeds
is like a garden full of weeds.

A rolling stone gathers no moss.

Action is eloquence.

Actions speak louder than words.

Activity is contagious.

An acre of performance is worth
the whole land of promise.

An idle mind is the devil's workshop.

An ounce of performance is
worth a ton of excuses.

Be a turtle; he makes progress
when he sticks his neck out.

Daily obedience is better than occasional sacrifice.

Decision determines destiny.

Delayed obedience is disobedience.

Destiny delayed is the devil's delight.

Diligence is the mother of good fortune.

Discouragement always follows
a decision to delay action.

"Do not love sleep or you will grow poor"
(Proverbs 20:13, *NIV*).

Do you have a backbone or a wishbone?

Doing nothing is in every man's power.

Doing nothing is the most tiresome
job because you can't stop and rest.

Don't wait for the hearse to take you to church.

Don't wait until you die to be brought to church.

"Even a child is known by his doings"
(Proverbs 20:11).

Even a fly doesn't get a slap on
the back until he starts to work.

Even if you're on the right track, you'll
get run over if you just sit there.

Every man's work is a portrait of himself.

Expect poison from standing water.

Find something you love to do and
you'll never work a day in your life.

God gives the nuts, but He does not crack them.

God helps those who help themselves.

God isn't looking for ability,
He's looking for availability.

Good intentions aren't good enough.

Great opportunities come to those
who make the most of small ones.

Happiness is a state of activity.

He who buries his talent is making a grave mistake.

Ideas have a short shelf life.

"Idle hands are the devil's workshop; idle lips are his mouthpiece" (Proverbs 16:27, *TLB*).

Idleness has poverty for wages.

Idleness is the root of all mischief.

If what you did yesterday still looks big to you, you haven't done much today.

If you're not going to put your quarter in the phone, get out of the booth.

In the life of one man, never the same time returns.

Inaction earns disrespect.

Initiative consists of doing the right thing without being told.

It is better to try something and fail than try nothing and succeed.

Kill procrastination, not time.

Knowing is not enough; we must apply.

Willing is not enough; we must do.

Laziness is often mistaken for patience.

Laziness travels so slowly that poverty soon overtakes it.

"Lazy men are soon poor; hard workers get rich" (Proverbs 10:4, *TLB*).

Lead, follow, or get out of the way!

Let him that would move the world, first move himself.

Life is like a coin. You can spend it however
you want, but you can only spend it once.

Maturity doesn't come with age; it comes with
acceptance of responsibility.

No man can do nothing, and
no man can do everything.

No one ever drowned in sweat!

No one ever stumbled into
something big while sitting down.

No one knows what he can do until he tries.

None are so busy as those who do nothing.

Not to have tried is the true failure.

Nothing ventured, nothing gained.

One action is more valuable than
a thousand good intentions.

One cannot waste time; he simply wastes his life.

"Only a fool idles away his time"
(Proverbs 12:11, *TLB*).

Opportunities take "now" for an answer.

Opportunity is missed by most people
because it looks like work.

Optimism without action is the philosophy of fools.

Perhaps the most important trip you will
ever make is going the second mile.

Plow deep while sluggards sleep.

Prepare and prevent instead of repair and repent.

Pressure follows procrastination.

Procrastination is the grave in
which opportunity is buried.

Procrastination is the thief of time.

Prolonged idleness paralyzes initiative.

Putting off a simple thing makes it hard;
putting off a hard thing makes it impossible.

Remember . . . it wasn't raining
when Noah built the ark.

Responsibility is the price of greatness.

Shallow men believe in luck; strong
men believe in cause and effect.

Small mounds of dirt add up to a mountain.

Some people find life an empty
dream because they put nothing into it.

Some people know all their rights,
but none of their obligations.

Some temptations come to the industrious,
but all temptations attack the idle.

The actions of men are the best
interpreters of their thoughts.

The answers to your prayers will include action.

The best preparation for tomorrow
is to do today's work superbly well.

The best way to predict the future is to create it.

The bias of nature is always toward the
wilderness, never toward the fruitful field.

The daily grind of hard work polishes a person.

The dictionary is the only place
where success comes before work.

The more we do, the more we can do.

The most important moment in your life is right now.

The only job where you start at
the top is digging a hole.

The smallest deed is better than
the greatest intention.

The time to repair the roof
is when the sun is shining.

The train of failure usually runs
on the track of laziness.

The way to get to the top is to get off your bottom.

The worst failure is failure to try.

Those who really want to do something find a way,
the others find excuses.

Thunder is impressive, but lightning does the work.

Triumph is just "umph" added to "try."

Trouble is usually produced by those
who produce nothing else.

We can do no great things—only
small things with great love.

We only attain in proportion to what we attempt.

What you plant now, you will harvest later.

When opportunity knocks, you must
get off your seat to open the door.

When we do what we can, God will do what we can't.

When you kill a little time, you
may be murdering opportunity.

When you're a self-starter, others
don't have to be a crank.

When you're through trying, you're through.

Words without actions are the assassins of dreams.

Yesterday is past, tomorrow may
never come; we have only today.

You cannot do everything, but you can do something.

You cannot enjoy life without contributing to it.

You can't enjoy the harvest
without laboring in the fields.

You can't get anywhere unless you start.

You can't make footprints in the
sand of time sitting down.

You draw nothing out of the bank
of life except what you deposit in it.

You will never find time for
anything; you must make it.

# LEADERSHIP

Christ is not the leader He could be if
you're not the follower you ought to be.

Confidence doesn't have all the answers,
but it is open to all the questions.

Every leader needs to make sure
he has some followers.

God doesn't need great men;
great men need God.

He that has learned to obey
will know how to command.

He that would govern others
must first govern himself.

If you don't live it, don't teach it.

If you think you are leading and no one
is following, you are only taking a walk.

If you want to be great, be the servant of all.

If you want to lead the orchestra,
you must turn your back on the crowd.

Leaders are readers.

Leadership is a relationship.

Management is doing things right;
leadership is doing the right thing.

To deny self is to become a nonconformist.
To get nowhere, follow the crowd.

# LIFE

A good life is a main argument.

As long as you live, keep learning how to live.

Believe that life is worth living and it will be.

Find something you love to do and
you'll never work a day in your life.

God's plan for your life is better than your own.

If you live wrong, you can't die right.

It is by acts and not by ideas that people live.

It is not death that a man should fear,
but never beginning to live.

It is not the years in your life but
the life in your years that counts.

Life is a promise; fulfill it.

Life is fragile; handle with prayer.

Life is like a coin. You can spend it however
you want, but you can only spend it once.

Life is more fun if you don't keep score.

Life is tragic for the person who has
plenty to live on but nothing to live for.

Life with Christ is an endless hope,
not a hopeless end.

Life's disappointments are opportunity's
hidden appointments.

Live among men as if God were looking;
speak to God as if men were listening.

Live as if you were to die tomorrow.

Live each day so that you will neither be afraid
of tomorrow nor ashamed of yesterday.

Live so that you wouldn't be ashamed
to sell the family parrot to the town gossip.

Live today what you want written in your epitaph.

Live your life as an exclamation, not an explanation.

Living above the circumstance is not by chance!

Living for Christ never gets easier, but it
does get better and better.

Miracles happen!

Some people find life an empty dream
because they put nothing into it.

Some people seem to know how to
live everybody's lives but their own.

The key to your future is hidden
in your daily approach to life.

The life that is unexamined is not worth living.

The life that is worth living is worth working for.

The life you live day-by-day is the
religion you truly possess.

The only sign of life is growth, and growth is change.

We need the Son to grow.

You can preach a better sermon
with your life than with your lips.

You cannot enjoy life without contributing to it.

Your life is what your thoughts make it.

# LOVE AND MARRIAGE

A full cabin is better than an empty castle.

A happy marriage is the union
of two good forgivers.

A happy marriage to another
requires a divorce from yourself.

A sense of humor is like a needle
and thread—it will patch many things.

A successful marriage isn't finding
the right person—it is being the right person.

Be courteous with all but intimate with few.

Compassion is love in action.

Don't ever slam the door;
you might want to go back.

Familiarity may not breed contempt,
but it takes off the edge of admiration.

Family happiness is homemade.

Faults are thin where love is thick.

God can heal a broken heart,
but He has to have all the pieces.

God may have made us different,
but He loves us the same.

God wants a whole heart,
but will keep a broken one.

God's love has been tried and found true.

"Hatred stirreth up strifes; but love
covereth all sins" (Proverbs 10:12).

Home is a place our feet may leave,
but not our heart.

Husband, wife and God—it's hard
to break a three-strand cord.

If the grass looks greener in
others' marriage, fertilize yours!

If you don't love yourself, you
can't possibly love your neighbor.

Keep thy eyes wide open before
marriage and half shut afterwards.

Keys to a good marriage: When you're wrong,
admit it. When you're right, shut up.

Leave everyone a little better than you found them.

"Bear one another's burdens" (Galatians 6:2, *NKJV*).

Life is tragic for the person who has plenty
to live on but nothing to live for.

Love and respect: You can't have a
healthy relationship without either one.

Love does not dominate; it cultivates.

Love doesn't keep score.

Love indeed is love in deed.

Love is a language anyone can speak.

Love is blind, and marriage is the eye-opener.

Love is blind; friendship closes its eyes.

Love is the art of hearts and heart of arts.

Love is the medicine for the sickness of the world.

Love is the tie that binds.

Love one another.

Love people and use things instead
of using people and loving things.

Love sees through a telescope, not a microscope.

Loved the wedding; invite Me
to the marriage.—God

Marriage is a marathon, not a sprint.

Marriage is our last, best chance to grow up.

Marriage may be made in heaven,
but the maintenance is done here on earth!

People don't care how much you know
until they know how much you care.

Put your spouse first so your marriage will last.

Putting God first makes your marriage last.

There are enough targets to aim at
without firing at each other.

They will know you are Christians by your love.

We can do no great things—only small
things with great love.

You can send your marriage to the
grave with a series of little digs.

Your heart has eyes that the brain knows nothing of.

# OPPORTUNITY

A pessimist sees difficulty in every opportunity;
an optimist sees opportunity in every difficulty.

A wise man will make more
opportunities than he finds. *15 MAR 2014*

An overcautious person burns bridges
of opportunity before he gets to them.

Big problems disguise big opportunities. *15 APR 2015*

Go out on a limb—that's where the fruit is.

God's best gifts are not things,
they are opportunities. *09 AUG 2014*

Great opportunities come to those
who make the most of small ones.

In the middle of difficulty lies opportunity.

Life's disappointments are
opportunity's hidden appointments.

Luck is what happens when
preparation meets opportunity.

No great man ever complains
of want of opportunity.

Opportunities are seldom labeled.

Opportunities can drop in your lap if you
have your lap where opportunities drop.

Opportunities take now for an answer.

Opportunity is often lost in the deliberation.

Opportunity is often missed
because it looks like work.

Opportunity knocks once, but temptation
stays at the door for years.

Procrastination is the grave in
which opportunity is buried.

Small opportunities are often the
beginning of great achievements.

The secret of success in life is to be
ready for opportunity when it comes.

The sign on the door of opportunity reads "Push."

There is no security on this earth—only opportunity.

Through indecision, opportunity is often lost.

Turn change into opportunity.

What we call adversity, God calls opportunity.

When opportunity knocks, you have
to get up and answer the door.

When you kill a little time, you
may be murdering opportunity.

Why don't we jump at opportunities
as quickly as we jump at conclusions?

# PARENTING

"A foolish man despises his mother"
(Proverbs 15:20).

A home without a Bible is like a
ship without a compass.

An ounce of mother is worth
more than a pound of clergy.

By the time we're experienced
at parenting, we're unemployed.

Children are like mirrors;
they reflect our attitudes in life.

Children follow parents' example
rather than their advice.

Children need love, especially
when they don't deserve it.

Children need models more than critics.

Children will follow your footsteps
quicker than your advice.

Don't let your parents down;
they brought you up.

Each day of our lives we make deposits
in the memory banks of our children.

Home is wherever Mom is.

"Honor your father and your mother"
(Exodus 20:12).

It is better to build a child than rebuild an adult.

It's hard to train up a child in the
way their parents didn't go.

Little children are a big concern to God.

Love and respect are the two most
important ingredients in parenting.

No worldly success can compensate
for failure at home.

Our children's character tomorrow is shaped
by what they learn from us today.

Parents are just baby-sitters for God.

Parents can tell but never teach,
until they practice what they preach.

Raising teenagers is like nailing Jell-O to a tree.

Some parents would rather their children
look like them than act like them.

Spend time, not just money, on your children.

Talk to God about your children;
talk to your children about God.

"Teach a child to choose the right path, and when he
is older he will remain upon it" (Proverbs 22:6, *TLB*).

Thank God for fathers who not only gave us life
but also taught us how to live.

"The best gift a father can give his children is
to love their mother" (Ephesians 5:25).

The best inheritance a father
can leave is a good example.

The cure for crime is not in the electric
chair but in the high chair.

The secret of dealing successfully
with a child is not to be his parent.

Two gifts to give your children: roots and wings.

You can have an ex-wife or an ex-husband,
but you can never have an ex-child.

# PATIENCE

A handful of patience is worth
more than a bushel of brains.

Better to be patient on the road
than a patient in the hospital.

Everyone has patience; successful
people learn to use it.

Everything is difficult before it is easy. 28FEB2015

Excellence is not a gift given, it is a skill perfected.

He that can have patience can have what he wills.

Hear much, speak little.

If you burn the candle at both ends
you are not as bright as you think.

If you pluck the blossoms,
you must do without the fruit.

Laziness is often mistaken for patience.

Make the best of it when you get the worst of it.

To be patient, you must learn patience.

Our patience will achieve more than our force.

Patience is a virtue that carries a lot of wait.

Patience is bitter but its fruit is sweet.

Patience is waiting without worrying.

Patience unlocks the door to achievement.

Perhaps the most important trip you will
ever make is going the second mile.

The secret of patience is to divert
your attention to something else.

Why is there not enough time to do a job right,
but always enough time to do it over?

Patience is the companion of wisdom.

Be as patient with others as God is with you.

# PERSEVERANCE

Be like the woodpecker: use your
head and keeping pecking!

By perseverance the snail reached the ark.

Failure is waiting on the path of least persistence.

Grow where you are planted.

If there is no wind, row.

If you want the rainbow, you gotta
put up with the rain.

In trying times, don't quit trying.

It is not the man with a motive
but the man with a purpose who prevails.

It's not how far you fall but how high
you bounce that makes the difference.

Keep on keeping on.

Perhaps the most important trip you will
ever make is going the second mile.

Perseverance is a strong will;
obstinacy is a strong won't.

The proof of desire is in the pursuit.

The whole ocean is made up of little drops.

Things turn out best for the people who make
the best of the way things turn out.

We get knocked down but not knocked out.

When faithfulness is most difficult,
it is most necessary.

When God stretches you, you never
snap back to your original shape.

# PRAYER

A Christian on his knees sees
more than the world on its tiptoes.

A church stays on its feet when its
members stay on their knees.

A day hemmed in prayer is less likely to unravel.

A life without prayer is powerless.

Anything worth worrying about
is worth praying about.

Are you quiet enough to hear God speak?

Arguments never settle things;
prayer changes things.

As long as there are tests, there will
always be prayer in public schools.

Backsliding begins when knee-bending ends.

Bending our knees in prayer keeps us
from breaking under the load of care.

Daily prayers will diminish your cares.

Don't ask God for what you think is good;
ask God for what He thinks is good for you.

Don't let adversity get you down,
except on your knees.

Don't pray for a bushel and only carry a cup.

Don't pray for rain if you're going to
complain about the mud.

Frequent prayers lessen daily cares.

Get an expert opinion, pray.

God will supply that for which we have knee'd.

God's answers are wiser than our prayers.

He who rises from his prayers a better man,
his prayers are answered.

He who walks upright must learn to kneel daily.

I can call on Jesus anytime; He is always on the line.

If prayer does not drive sin out of
your life, sin will drive prayer out.

If you can't sleep, don't count
sheep—talk to the Shepherd.

Instead of waiting on the Lord,
some expect the Lord to wait on them.

Kneeling is the proper posture for
putting seeds in the ground.

Kneeling keeps you in good standing with God.

Let us bear one another's burdens.

Life is fragile, handle with prayer.

Live among men as if God were looking;
speak to God as if men were listening.

Morning prayer leads to evening praise.

Most people have too little prayer and
too much propaganda.

Never face a day until you have prayed.

No one can live wrong and pray right.

No one is poor who can by prayer
open the storehouse of God.

Nothing makes us love our enemies
as much as praying for them.

Peace of mind depends on strength of mind.

Pray hardest when it's hardest to pray.

Prayer does not change God,
it changes the one who prays.

Prayer is a way of life not just an emergency detour.

Prayer is asking for rain,
faith is carrying the umbrella.

Prayer is not a way to get what we want
but to become what God wants us to be.

Prayer is the pause that empowers.

Prayer is the tool to talk to the one who rules.

Prayer lubricates the machinery of life.

Prayer need not be long when faith is strong.

Prayer should be the key of the
morning and the lock of the night.

Reach new heights by getting on your knees.

Satan laughs at our toiling, mocks our
wisdom, but trembles when we pray.

Satan trembles when he sees
the weakest saint upon his knees.

Serving God is like playing golf—keep your
knees bent and your arms extended.

Seven days without prayer makes one weak.

Stay on your knees before God and
on your feet before men.

Step by step, prayer by prayer,
God will always get you there.

Study hard for school; pray hard for life.

The answers to your prayers will include action.

The only way to walk without falling is on your knees.

The secret to praying is praying in secret.

To hear the call of God, one must
be within hearing distance.

To walk with God, we must talk with God.

Too often we pray for a change in our
circumstances instead of a change in our character.

Turn care into prayer anywhere.

When it seems hardest to pray, pray hardest!

When praying, do not give God
instructions to report for duty.

When we pray for rain we must be willing
to put up with a little mud.

When we tap into God's eternal power
our resources are limitless.

Which way did you begin your day . . .
with prayer or without it?

Why worry when you can pray?

You never stand taller than
when you kneel before God.

You will never get a busy signal
on the prayer line to heaven.

# PRIDE

A candle lights others and consumes itself.

A good man is always willing to be little.

A man who refuses to admit his mistakes
can never be successful.

He who toots his own horn soon has
everybody dodging when he approaches.

A man wrapped up in himself makes a
very small package.

A person who knows everything
has the most to learn.

A prideful person never gets anywhere,
because he thinks he's already there.

Are you quiet enough to hear God speak?

Conscience is the still small voice
that makes you feel still smaller.

Don't talk about yourself,
it will be done when you leave.

Everyone is better than someone else,
and not as good as someone else.

God can't indwell in someone
who is full of themselves.

He that boasts of his own knowledge
proclaims his ignorance.

He who falls in love with himself,
will have no rivals.

He who is full of himself,
is likely to be quite empty.

Hold your head up but keep
your nose at a friendly level.

"Humble yourselves in the sight of the Lord
and He shall lift you up" (James 4:10).

If you think you've arrived, you'll be left behind.

In the race for excellence there is no finish line.

Is God finished with you yet?

It is easier to be honest with others
than it is to be honest with yourself.

It is easy to see through people who
make spectacles of themselves.

It is impossible for a man to learn
what he thinks he already knows.

It's better to ask some questions
than to know all the answers

"He must increase, but I must decrease"
(John 3:30).

Lord make me humble so that I may not stumble.

Many complain of their memory,
but few of their judgment.

Noble deeds concealed are most esteemed.

None are so empty as those
who are full of themselves.

Nothing sets a person so much
out of the devil's reach as humility.

People can't see eye to eye with you
if you are looking down on them.

People seldom improve when they have
no model but themselves to copy.

"Pride goes before destruction"
(Proverbs 16:18, *NKJV*).

Remember, you're an original,
just like everybody else.

Temper can get you into trouble,
but pride will keep you there.

The banana that gets away from
the bunch gets peeled and eaten.

The entire population, with one
exception, is composed of others.

The first test of a truly great man is his humility.

The man who thinks he knows it all
has merely stopped thinking.

Tunnel vision tells you nobody
is working as hard as you are.

When you talk, you repeat what you already know;
when you listen, you learn.

Why do people who know the least,
know it the loudest?

# SERVICE AND COMMITMENT

A man of words and not of deeds
is like a garden full of weeds.

Actions speak louder than words.

Are you living a life that matters
in terms of time and eternity?

Availability is the greatest ability you have.

Be a candle if you cannot be a lighthouse.

Delayed obedience is disobedience.

Doing the will of God leaves no
time to dispute His plans.

Don't be afraid to go out on a limb.
That's where the fruit is.

Don't go through life; grow through life.

Don't run with the world, walk with God.

Faithfulness in little things is a great thing.

Find something you love to do and
you'll never work a day in your life.

Floating members make a sinking church.

Forget yourself for others and
others will not forget you.

God is not seeking compliments, but commitments.

God isn't looking for ability;
He's looking for availability.

He who begins too much, accomplishes little.

He who lends to the poor gets his interest from God.

If you want to defend Christianity, practice it.  21 SEPT 2014

If your religion doesn't take you to church,
it's doubtful it will take you to heaven.

Initiative consists of doing the
right thing without being told.

Integrity is Christlike character in working clothes.

It is not the man with a motive but the
man with a purpose who prevails.

Judge this day not by the harvest
but by the seeds planted.

Knowing Scripture is one thing;
knowing the Author is another

Nominal Christians follow Christ,
but not too closely or too literally.

Obedience brings blessings.

Once you've found a better way,
make that way better.

One heart dedicated to God
can bring light to the world.

Only one life and it soon will pass;
only what's done for Christ will last.

Real generosity is doing something nice
for someone who'll never find it out.

Some people know Christ; some
just know about Him!

Teaching is a work of heart.

The actions of men are
the best interpreters of thoughts.

The best way to progress is to help
the man ahead of you get promoted.

The church is not a dormitory for sleepers,
it is an institution for workers.

The church is not a waiting room for saints,
it is a hospital for sinners.

The more you pour out, the more He pours in.

Those who really want to do something
find a way, the others find excuses.

To be an atheist requires more faith
than to be a Christian.

To walk in your own way is to run away from God.

What on earth are you doing for heaven's sake? 17 mar 2015

When you're a self-starter,
others don't have to be a crank.

Willingness is not enough; we must do.

With every deed you are sowing a seed
though the harvest you may not see.

You can't enjoy the harvest without
laboring in the fields.

160

You were created to be an answer.

Your feelings will always catch up
to your commitment.

Your life makes a difference.

# SOCIAL ISSUES

A radical is anyone whose
opinion is different from yours.

Abortion is advocated only by persons
who have themselves been born.

As long as there are tests, there will
always be prayer in public schools.

Be certain your feet are planted in the
right place before you decide to stand firm.

Be open minded . . . but not so open
minded your brains fall out.

Christian's aren't perfect . . . just forgiven.

Drinking is committing suicide
on the installment plan.

Freedom is the right to be wrong,
not the right to do wrong.

He who lends to the poor
gets interest from God.

If you want to defend Christianity, practice it.

Injustice anywhere is a
threat to justice everywhere.

It is impossible to govern the world
without God and the Bible.

It's better to light a candle than curse the darkness.

It's easier to abstain than refrain.

Men are not against you,
they are merely for themselves.

Minds are like parachutes,
they function only when open.

Minds, like streams, may be so
broad that they're shallow.

Public opinion is not the voice of God.

Red and yellow, black and white,
we are all precious in His sight.

Right is right even if everybody's against it
and wrong is wrong even if everybody's for it.

The Bible describes "safe sex" as marriage.

The Bible is your best TV guide.

The world at its worst needs a church at its best.

True religion is never solitary.

Trust God's authority, not man's majority.

We cannot win the war against injustice
until we win the war against apathy.

What is popular is not always right;
what is right is not always popular.

You can't hide from God by missing church.

# SUCCESS

Ten ways to reach your goal: 1. Persevere
2. Forget the rest, you won't need them.

A goal is a dream without a deadline.

A minute's success pays the failure of years.
—Robert Browning

A successful person can lay a firm
foundation with the bricks others throw at him.

A successful person continues to look
for work even after he has a job.

All progress is due to those who were
not satisfied to leave well enough alone.

Always begin with the end in mind.

Always imitate the behavior of the
winners when you lose.—George Meredith

Being a hero is about the shortest lived
profession on earth.—Will Rogers

Beware lest your footprints in the sands of time
leave only the marks of a heel.

Big shots are just little shots that kept shooting.
—Christopher Morley

Birds fly in flocks, but eagles fly alone.

Build momentum by accumulating small successes.

Choose friends who pull you up, not drag you down.

Clear your mind of "can't."

Diligence is the mother of good fortune.

Don't be afraid to go out on a limb.
That's where the fruit is.

Don't ever slam the door; you might want to go back.

Don't just go on to other things,
go on to higher things.

Don't let what you cannot do interfere
with what you can.

Don't worry about knowing people,
make yourself worth knowing.

Enthusiasm is the most important
ingredient of success.

Envy provides the mud that failures throw at success.

Even when opportunity knocks, you
must get off your seat to open the door.

Every accomplishment great or
small begins with a decision.

Every calling is great when greatly pursued.
—Oliver Wendell Holmes

Every man's work is a portrait of himself.

Everyone has patience; successful
people learn to use it.

Everything is difficult before it is easy.

Excellence is not a gift given, it is a skill perfected.

Experience is the name we give to our mistakes.

Experience may make a person knowledgeable;
but only God can make a person wise.

Fear of criticism is the kiss of death in
the courtship of achievement.

Find something you love to do and you'll
never work a day in your life.

Goals are like stars; even if not reached they can
always be a guide.

God doesn't call us to be successful; He calls us
to be faithful.—Albert Hubbard

God's resources are always
equal to His requirements.

Great opportunities come to those
who make the most of small ones.

Those who learn to obey know how to command.

Those who stay in the valley never get over the hill.

Those who bury their talents make a grave mistake.

Those who do not sacrifice are not likely to succeed.

He will not have a barren mind who
knows how to bear in mind.

If at first you do succeed, try something harder.

If you cannot do great things, do small
things in a great way.

If you have no critics you likely have no successes.
—Malcom Forbes

If you never stick your neck out,
you'll never get above the crowd.

If you refuse to admit your mistakes,
you can never be successful.

If you want to be great, be the servant of all.

If you want to lead the orchestra,
you must turn your back on the crowd.

If your head sticks above the crowd,
expect more stones to be thrown at you.

In order to be irreplaceable, one
must always be different.

In the race for excellence there is no finish line.

It is better to ask twice than lose your way once.

It isn't your position that makes you
happy but your disposition.

Joy is spiritual prosperity.

Judge this day not by the harvest
but by the seeds planted.

Many of life's failures did not realize how close
they were to success when they gave up.
—Thomas Edison

Many receive advice, the wise profit by it.

Maturity doesn't come with age, it comes
with acceptance of responsibility.

Most successes are built on failures.

No destination is beyond the reach
of one who walks with God.

No worldly success can compensate
for failure at home.

Only those who dare to fail greatly can ever
achieve greatly.—Robert Kennedy

Position doesn't make one happy;
disposition makes one happy.

Remain indecisive and you will never grow.

Responsibility is the price of greatness.
—Winston Churchill

Satan always attacks those who
can hurt him the most.

Shallow men believe in luck, successful
men believe in cause and effect.—Emerson

Small opportunities are often the
beginning of great achievements.

Success comes in cans; failure comes in cant's.

Success depends more on energy and drive than it
does on intelligence.—Sloan Wilson

Success doesn't eliminate obstacles,
it creates new ones.

Success is a matter of holding on
after others have let go.

Success is doing common things uncommonly well.

Success lies in the person, not in the job.

The "Man of the Hour" spent many
days and nights getting there.

The best way to progress is to help
the man ahead of you get promoted.

The creation of a thousands forests is in one acorn.
—Ralph Waldo Emerson

The dictionary is the only place
where "success" comes before "work."

The difference between ordinary and
extraordinary is that little extra.—Zig Ziglar

The enemy always attacks those in the front lines.

The first requisite in success is the ability to pick good people.—Lee Lacocca

The greatest ability in business is to get along with others.—John Hancock

The higher you go the more dependent you become on other people.

The person who doesn't need a boss is usually the one selected to be one.

The real secret of success is enthusiasm.—Walter Chrysler

The really great person is the person who makes every person feel great.

The secret of success is constancy to purpose.—Benjamin Disraeli

The secret of success is to be ready for opportunity when it comes.—Disraeli

The secret of success is to do common things uncommonly well.—Rockefeller

The sky's not the limit.

The virtue of achievement is victory over oneself.

The way to get to the top is to get off your bottom.

There is no such thing as great talent without great willpower.

Those who never succeed themselves are always eager to tell you how.

To avoid criticism say nothing, do nothing, and be nothing.

To move on from where you are,
decide where you want to be.

Triumph is just "umph" added to "try."

Trust in the invisible to do the impossible.

Try not to become a man of success, but rather try
to become a man of value.—Albert Einstein

We will think and talk like the
person we listen to the most.

Winners simply do what losers don't want to do.

Wisdom begins with wonder.

You always pass failure on the way to success.

You can always tell a failure by
the way he criticizes success.

You can reach greater heights
if you have more depth.

# TIME

Be jealous of your time,
it's your greatest treasure.

God is worth your time.

God's timing is always perfect.

He's an "on time" God.

If you burn the candle at both ends,
you are not as bright as you think.

Invest time in improving yourself
instead of disapproving in others.

Lost time is never found.

Nothing valuable can be lost by taking time.

Something dominates everyone's day.

Stress usually accompanies us when
we are out of pace with God.

The best preparation for tomorrow
is to do today's work well.

The most important moment in
your life is right now.

The place to be happy is here;
the time to be happy is now.

The recipe for a good speech
includes some shortening.

The unwise person seeks happiness in the future,
the wise person grows it today.

Time and words can never be recalled.

Time wasted is existence; time used is life.

Today is a gift . . . that's why
it's called "the present."   15 MAR 2015

Why is there never enough time to do a job
right, but always enough time to do it over?

Yesterday is past . . . tomorrow may
never come . . . we have only today.

You will never "find" time for anything.

If you want time you must make it.

You will never have this moment again.

"Few sinners are saved after the first 20
minutes of a sermon."—Mark Twain